About the Authors

Andrew Bondy (@andrewpbondy) was born in Windsor, Ontario, to a man and woman who will buy more copies of this book than you can imagine. He is married to a lovely woman (Chelsea) and indentured to a tiny bulldog (Beans). When not performing with his 1980s CanCon Rock Quartet (Michael Xero), he rides his bike around Toronto and does some light mechanical engineering. Andrew continues to seek out the mysteries of Canada, ever searching for the perfect Tim Hortons tea biscuit.

Julia Davidovich (@juliadavidovich) is a writer who sports an impressively large top knot in order to avoid washing her hair. Julia is originally from Toronto and currently resides in Los Angeles with her husband, Jon, and their cat-children, Francis and Roxy. Despite living in Canada's underpants, Julia strives to make sure every playlist she creates contains over 35% of her CanCon favourites.

Sam Montgomery (@sammontgomery) is the youngest person to ever win five Juno awards. She cherishes spending time with her mother (Meryl Streep) and casting spells with her coven. When she's not drinking wine with her best friends, Jessica Chastain, Julianne Moore, and Amy Adams, she enjoys listening to Motown and cooking with her husband, Anderson Cooper, and their many rescue dogs.

Eric Taylor (@erictaylorswift) is often mistaken for Ray's brother from *Everybody Loves Raymond*—he is not. His wife, Melinda, has been recommended for sainthood for not only marrying Eric, but also being the mother to their lovely daughter. Eric aspires to one day binge watch every season of *Murdoch Mysteries*.

150 Years of STATS Canada!

A GUIDE TO CANADA'S GREATEST COUNTRY

From the experts behind the Twitter sensation
@stats_canada

PENGUIN

an imprint of Penguin Canada, a division of Penguin Random House Canada Limited

Canada • USA • UK • Ireland • Australia • New Zealand • India • South Africa • China

First published 2017

www.penguinrandomhouse.ca

Library and Archives Canada Cataloguing in Publication

150 years of Stats Canada! : a guide to Canada's greatest country.

From the experts behind the Twitter sensation @STATS_CANADA.

ISBN 978-0-7352-3280-8 (paperback)
ISBN 978-0- 7352-3281-5 (electronic)

1. National characteristics, Canadian—Humor. 2. Canada—Civilization—Humor. 3. Canada—Statistics—Humor. 4. Satire, Canadian (English). 5. Twitter. I. Title: One hundred fifty years of Stats Canada!. II. Title: One hundred and fifty years of Stats Canada!. III. @STATS_CANADA (Twitter account).

FC173.A15 2017   971.07   C2016-906947-8

Cover and interior design: Leah Springate
Cover images: (moose) CSA Images/Getty Images; (plaid) Wiktoria Pawlak/Shutterstock.com

Printed and bound in the United States of America

10 9 8 7 6 5 4 3 2 1

Contents

Introduction   1

150 Things to See and Do in Canada

Pack Your Luggage   6

Download Canadian Apps   8

Consider the Canadian Hierarchy
of Needs   10

Buy Canada a Birthday Present   11

Convert Things to Canadian   12

Learn About Canadian Currency   14

Visit Every CFL Stadium   16

Go Shopping   18

Visit New Brunswick   20

Complete the Five Feats of Ne'erbrun   21

Hike the Bruce Trail   22

Find Out Which Canadian Music You
Should Listen To   23

Score a Canadian Hat Trick   24

Take a Domestic Flight   26

Pass the Citizenship Test   28

Text Like a Canadian   30

Read the Tim Hortons Wi-Fi Terms and
Conditions   31

Visit Quebec   32

Learn About Quebec's Famous Battles   34

Get to Know Gatineau!   35

Have a Montreal Bachelor Party   36

Cure a Canadian Hangover   39

Pick a Side: Leafs vs. Habs   40

Learn Quebec's Most-Used Phrases   41

Learn Tim Hortons Etiquette   42

Hack the Tim Hortons "Secret Menu"   44

Avoid Dying in Ontario   45

Go to TIFF   46

Visit an ONroute   48

Experience Ontario's Nature   49

Have Fun on Lake Ontario   50

Get Told Off in Toronto   52

See a Blue Jays Game   53

Rent an Apartment in Toronto   54

Visit Paris, Ontario   56

Visit Dryden's Art Gallery   57

Enjoy a Craft Beer from Every Province   58

Dodge the Draft   60

Cut Your Hair Like Wayne Gretzky   61

Visit Alberta   62

Get an Alberta-Themed Tattoo   66

Get to Know Calgary   67

Attend the Calgary Stampede   68

Contents

Fit In in Alberta   69

Visit the Drumheller Dinosaur Museum   70

Get Health Insurance in Your Province or Territory   72

Learn About Canadian Snowmobile Demographics   73

Visit Manitoba   74

Drive Safe in Manitoba   75

Fix Climate Change   76

Experience Car Trouble   78

Give a ZED Talk   79

Spend a Day with the Queen   80

Get to Know Boomer   81

Discover Saskatchewan   82

Visit the Saskatoon Wheat King   84

Match the Saskatchewan Resource with Its Use   85

Visit the Fictional Birthplace of Canada's Favourite Redhead   86

Visit the Potato Museum   88

Risk Hypothermia in the Canadian Territories   90

Sample a Few CanCon Favourites at the Hard Rocque Café   92

Get to Know Trooper   94

Meet the Real Houseboatwives of Snout Harbour, NFLD   95

Have Your Expectations Exceeded   96

Learn the Differences Between Stephen Harper and Justin Trudeau   97

Hop on the *Just for Laughs* Death Tour   98

Beat the MuchMusic Video Dance Party Escape Room   100

Discover the Secret Messages in Fred Penner's Songs   102

Celebrate iCal-uit's Subtle Name Change   103

"Get Lost" at the Magnetic Triangle   104

Learn Your Gords   105

Visit the Notable Canadian–American Wax Museum   106

Pick Up a Copy of Canada's Steamiest Hockey Erotica Series   108

Visit the Famous Five Statue at Parliament Hill   110

Eat a Donair: A How-To Guide   112

Bring Back Souvenirs from the Maritimes   113

Get Invited to a Cottage   114

Discover Canadian Wildlife   116

Visit the Abandoned Shania Twain Centre   118

Read a Forgotten Heather's Pick   120

Search the Web, Canadian Style   121

Visit Alberta's Gopher Hole Museum   122

Tell Someone Ellen Page Is from Nova Scotia   123

See Someone Who Was on *Degrassi*   124

Try Every Type of Poutine   125

Read a Forgotten Buzzfeed Canada Article   126

Have a Million Dollars (2017 Update)   127

Things Whiter Than Newfoundland   128

Have It Your Way at Harvey's   129

Take the Bus Instead   130

Ask for the Prime Minister's Special   132

Learn to Love Saskatchewan   134

Repurpose the Rideau Canal   135

Play a Game of High School Ringette   136

Watch Canadian Television   138

Play the *Chopped Canada* Drinking Game   140

Watch Canadian Netflix   141

Attend a Canadian University   142

Celebrate the Canadian Holidays   144

Learn Canadian Baseball   146

Become a Raccoon Whisperer   148

Attend the Bordertown Olympics   150

Diagnose Yourself with Web EhMD   151

Bundle Your Services with Rogers   152

Breed a Canadian Dog   154

Visit British Columbia   156

Buy a House in Vancouver   158

Unlock the Hidden Pub in Gastown, BC   159

Grow Old in Canada   160

Visit the Property Brothers' First Flip   162

Enjoy Canada's Greatest Resource: Dipping Sauce   163

Become Prime Minister   164

Memorize the Prime Ministers   168

Get Yourself a Custom NHL Jersey   169

Host a Canadian Dinner Party   170

Learn the Origins of Canadian Place Names   172

Celebrate Canadian Thanksgiving   173

Observe Canadian Law   174

See a Cover Band   175

Become a Billionaire   176

Play Toronto Maple Leafs Bingo   178

Contents

Visit the Newfoundland Iceberg
Museum   179

Dress Like a Canadian   180

Save the Village from the White Witch of
Saskatoon   182

Get a Prince Albert Piercing in Prince Albert,
Saskatchewan!   184

Trade in a Juno   185

Relate to Millennials   186

Feel Superior to America   187

Meet This Guy in Cole Harbour Who
Watched Sidney Crosby Play Once   188

Enjoy a PC Decadent Cookie   189

Discover How Fluent in French You Really
Are   190

Play a Canadian Drinking Game   192

Identify a Canadian Puck Boy   193

Visit the Queen's Secret Corgi Farm   194

Take Your Shoes Off at the Front
Door   196

Learn the Differences Between Bryan and
Ryan Adams   197

Meet the Feral Children Who Live in the
West Edmonton Mall   198

Defend Yourself from a Canada
Goose   200

Get a Canadian Arts Council Grant   201

Become a Lacrosse Fan   202

Keep Fit and Have Fun   204

Smoke Some Weed   205

Get a Better Phone Plan   206

Listen to a Canadian Playlist   208

Listen to One Rush Song   209

Dress Up for Halloween   210

Meet Ogopogo   211

Check Out Michael Cera's Speed Dial   212

Learn About Justin Trudeau's Alternative
Careers   213

Take the Quiz: How Canadian Are
You?   214

Conclusion: Save Canada   216

Acknowledgments   218

Art Credits   220

The stats team would like to dedicate this book to all the Twitter followers,
bad hockey teams, terrible politicians, and inclement weather
that made @stats_canada what it is today.

When the Fathers of Confederation gathered in Charlottetown 150 years ago, could they have imagined the Canada of 2017? Would they be awed by the skyscrapers of our great cities, the vast and productive wheat fields of our prairies, the critically acclaimed but commercially overlooked sophomore album by Carly Rae Jepsen? Did they have any inkling that, a century and a half hence, Canadians would look back at the architects of our independent dominion and think, "I have no clue who most of those old white dudes are"? Would they enjoy poutine?

The Canada of today is a thriving nation that encompasses six time zones, seven NHL teams, and the chance to win one of eight incredible grand prizes in this year's Roll Up the Rim sweepstakes. The maple leaf is recognized abroad as a symbol of tolerance, progressive ideas, and designer winter coats. Although the world may view Canada as a land of short summers and long underwear, we know it to be a complex, diverse country full of contradictions and conflicting visions: there's French Canada vs. English Canada, Ski-Doo Canada vs. Polaris Canada, and Chad Kroeger Canada vs. Gord Downie Canada, to name a few.

Over the last .15 kiloyears, Canada has changed dramatically. What was once a sparsely populated territory dominated by nature's hostility has been tamed by a single highway. The Atlantic and Pacific coasts are knit together by a cell phone monopoly. Pollution and liberal arts grads pour out of our modern cities.

The way Canadians earn their livings has changed, too: since 1867, the number of fur trappers has plummeted while the number of YouTube celebrities has increased significantly. Lumberjacks have moved away from the woods and into the artisanal coffee shops. A Canadian even went to live on the International Space Station and was kind of a real showboat about it.

To mark this important milestone, Stats Canada undertook an unprecedented survey of the country in its 150th year. With the blessing of our hunky new prime minister, the long-form census was retrieved from the recycling bin and our enumerators were allowed out of the basement and onto your doorstep. We fanned out across the terrain, from Ottawa to Nottawa, and recorded everything we saw: every fresh batch of Beaver Tails, every moose elected mayor of a small town, every sweater vest in the gift shop of the Stephen Harper Museum of Pseudoscience and Oil Pipelines. What emerged was a picture of a nation that is definitely one of North America's top three countries.

Along the way, we unearthed some surprising things (to mention just two, there's a heretofore undiscovered region of feudalism and magic sandwiched between Quebec and Nova Scotia called Ne'erbrun, and virtually every community in the land is home to a spooky abandoned museum). Whether you're just visiting or you've been swaddled in flannel your entire life, we're certain that this book will help you enjoy the very best this country has to offer.

We've converted our research into a definitive list of 150 things to see and do in Canada. Touching on every aspect of Canadian life, no inukshuk has been left unturned. As you enjoy the additional six weeks of paid holiday provided to all citizens* in celebration of the country's major milestone, let this book be your guide.

Differences Between 1867 Settlers and Canadians Today

Category	1867 Settlers	Today
Cuisine	Cheese, milk directly from the cow, whatever you hunt	Artisanal cheeses, craft beers, Uber Eats
Fashion	Bearded, plaid, leather boots	Bearded, plaid, leather boots (see fig. 1, over)
Jobs	Farming, fishing, shipbuilding, lumber	Your parents don't get what it is you do
Travel across country	Expensive and cumbersome	Expensive and cumbersome
How cute is the prime minister?	Wouldn't kiss him with someone else's lips	10 out of 10 would bang
Forms of entertainment	Drinking, sports, bragging about fish you caught	Drinking, sports, bragging about Facebook likes
Treatment of First Nations people	Not great!	Not great!
Will the Leafs win a Cup?	Not any time soon!	Definitely next season!
Is winter coming?	Yes	Yes

* Offer not valid in Quebec.

fig. 1

150 Things to See and Do in

_____

_____

_____

_____

Canada

Pack Your Luggage

Canadians spend approximately 36% of their waking hours talking about the weather, which translates into roughly 2,100 hours a year, per person, or 14 Rush songs. As the old Canadian rap song goes, "Weather rules everything around me" (W.R.E.A.M.). It controls the activities we do, shaping our national identity and making dressing for it extremely difficult. While this may be no surprise to a Canadian, to any tourist visiting our nation it can make packing a suitcase a nearly impossible task. They just don't make suitcases large enough to account for Canadian weather.

As part of our efforts to boost domestic tourism, we at Stats Canada have produced this guide to packing for a trip to Canada. A guide that will have you covered from coast to coast and from head to toe.

PACKING TIP: You can never have enough plaid or denim. Look in your suitcase and count the number of denim pieces. Now multiply by four. Does your underwear not have a plaid pattern? Wasted opportunity.

PACKING TIP: Put a Canadian flag patch on your backpack or carry-on so that people will think you're a Canadian returning home and not an American coming over to take advantage of our weak dollar.

PACKING TIP: Once you've arrived in Canada, dress every day like you're trying to avoid paying to check a bag at the airport. Layer, layer, layer. You should have more layers than an episode of *Degrassi: The Next Generation*. You never know when the morning will start off warm and sunny and end in snowflakes. Yes, even in August. Yes, it's nuts, we know. How do we deal with it? That's probably why our beer is so much stronger.

PACKING TIP: Don't forget your Blue Jays hat. Nothing has united our country more than cheering on the Blue Jays. Well, except for cheering against the Leafs. [*Editor's Note:* If anybody starts a conversation about the finer points of baseball, quickly change the subject.]

PACKING TIP: Try to leave space in your suitcase so that you can smuggle home ketchup chips and Kinder Surprises.

Tourists should also account for differing fashion trends from province to

1867 John A. Macdonald becomes first prime minister by being in right place at right time

province. Although Ski-Doo jackets may be popular in Duck Lake, Saskatchewan, they won't pass much muster in Happy Valley–Goose Bay, Newfoundland, where T-shirts found in cases of beer are still all the rage. Your flannel and cowboy boots may have been a hit at the bar during the Calgary Stampede, but wearing the same outfit among Toronto hipsters will have them laughing so hard they'll spit their $8 pint of craft beer out their noses. Basically, there's no way to win them all (you're not the Oilers in the 80s). Pick a style that works for you and go with it. You'll still be better dressed than Justin Bieber.

PACKING TIP: Quebec is actually very different from France. Wearing a striped shirt and a beret while clutching a baguette will have Montrealers thinking you're a mime or really early for Halloween or, worst of all, actually from France. The only thing the people of Quebec hate more than the rest of Canada is people actually from France.

PACKING TIP: When in Toronto, try to wear something from Drake's fashion line. Sure, a little expensive, but it'll pay off when you're getting that special

nod from trendy millennials, girls from Ryerson University, high school students from Scarborough, and an older woman who read about it in *The Globe and Mail.*

Above all, just have fun with it. Known for our great food, fun destinations, awesome beer, love of hockey, plethora of pop singers [*Editor's Note:* This list continued for another three pages and has been edited for brevity's sake], we are, however, not known for our sense of style. It's hard to be stylish while dressing for weather that is most reminiscent of the ice planet Hoth. Even Luke wore that dorky visor thing.

And remember, a Canadian tuxedo is not out of style; it's cool, comfortable, and the official uniform for 83% of Canadian dads.

1868 First official horse death in Canada

Download Canadian Apps

iTrudes

Are you tired of the same old negative, depressing songs? Featuring a beautiful design that puts style over substance, iTrudes automatically purges your library of pessimistic numbers and replaces them with sunshiny rhythms and upbeat choruses. It costs a lot more than most music services, but it's worth it—trust us!*

Maps: Snowmobile Edition

Find the nearest trails and the sickest jumps. Now featuring turn-by-turn navigation to the beer store.

Courteous Birds

This game of skill and dexterity pits you against a gang of rude American pigs. You win by holding the door open, saying "Bless you" to strangers, and not correcting somebody when they mispronounce your name.

---

* In 2015, Canadians were horrified when iTrudes rolled out an update that automatically synced an exclusive Sophie Trudeau Canadian covers album onto every user library.

Am I in Quebec?

Do the confusing signs and strange street buskers have you suddenly concerned that you've wandered over the Quebec border? This app is the only way to find out for sure.

SnapChad

This fun and flirty app adds a greasy mullet and pubescent goatee to all your sexy photos. Look at this photograph: it's me, but grosser!

Polkaroo Go

Experience the excitement of augmented reality as you embark on a real-world treasure hunt for the elusive Polkaroo. Follow the clues and keep searching; you're sure to find him someday. It's so much fun that you'll be saying, "Polkaroo was here? And I missed him again!?"

1869 First hipster appears in Toronto's west end

Consider the Canadian Hierarchy of Needs

SELF-ACTUALIZATION:
your team winning
the Stanley Cup

ESTEEM NEEDS:
owning a good snow shovel

LOVE NEEDS:
good feelings about the Queen

SAFETY NEEDS:
house that keeps out moose

PHYSIOLOGICAL NEEDS:
steady stream of Tim Hortons coffee pumping through veins

1870 Manitoba enters Confederation; remains a secret until 1959

Buy Canada a Birthday Present

On July 1, 2017, Canada celebrates its 150th birthday and you're invited to the party! You don't want to show up empty-handed, so here are some great gift suggestions for the classy old nation that doesn't look a day over 135.

A New Airport
Every nation wishes it had a new airport or two, but other expenses always get in the way. Why not treat Canada to a shiny new terminal and go halvsies with your siblings on the runways?

iTrudes Gift Card
Canada is still listening to old cassettes from the CBC archives. Surprise Canada with an iTrudes gift card entitling every citizen to one copy of Shania Twain's 2002 album *Up*.

Coupon for a Free Back Massage
Doing the heavy lifting for NATO can be exhausting. Show your country how much you care with a thoughtful, handwritten coupon redeemable for a sumptuous 12-minute massage.

$20
The long-time favourite of grandmas and aunts everywhere, a wrinkled $20 bill carefully folded into a Garfield-themed birthday card is a time-tested birthday gift guaranteed to please.

Alaska
Nothing would make Canada happier than to finally receive Alaska. Canada has been too polite to ask for it, but everybody sees the way Canada wistfully gazes over the Rockies at Alaska's long panhandle. We hear that America will trade it for sole custody of a sexy Ryan (Reynolds or Gosling). This year, let's give Canada the gift of a contiguous arctic frontier.

A Shirt for the Prime Minister
After Stephen Harper spent tens of thousands of dollars on election-year sweaters, the PMO's clothing budget has been slashed and Justin Trudeau has been forced to holiday shirtless. It's getting a bit nippy out there, so let's all chip in and get the guy a shirt.

An NFL Team We Can Ignore
Toronto won't be taken seriously as a major North American city until it has an NFL team to be indifferent about. If it doesn't work out, we can always give it back to Buffalo next Christmas.

One of Those Expensive Bay Blankets
You know, the kind you threw away when you were cleaning out your grandma's apartment a few years ago.

1871 Canada reaches peak moustache

Convert Things to Canadian

When travelling in Canada, the average tourist will be confused by many of the models Canadians use to determine such things as distance, cost, temperature, and musical aptitude. Visitors can be found asking "How many gallons is a milk bag?" or "What exactly are the Juno Awards?"

We present a helpful conversion list to assist our foreign guests.

1 mile = 1.609 kilometres (or average distance between Tim Hortons franchises)

Tourist: The mile markers on this highway are confusing and I don't feel like another coffee.

Canadian: Just three more Tim's and we'll just about be there, bud. Let's stop for a double-double.

1 dollar = 1 loonie (except for when the dollar is really bad)

Tourist: It says this bag of milk is four dollars. Really, it comes in bags here?

Canadian: Four loonies for a bag of milk—what a bargain!

32 Fahrenheit = 0 Celsius

Tourist: Wow, it's really cold. It's 43 degrees Fahrenheit!

Canadian: Sorry, no. This isn't cold. Want to hear about cold? Let me tell you about the winter of 2013.

1 gallon = 3.78 litres

Tourist: Drake cries approximately three gallons of tears a year thinking about exes who have wronged him.

Canadian: Drake cries approximately 11.35 litres of tears a year thinking about exes who have wronged him.

President = Prime Minister

Tourist: Donald Trump is the first pile of sentient garbage serving as president of the United States.

Canadian: Stephen Harper was Canada's first robot prime minister.

Grammy = Juno

Tourist: Nickelback have won 0 Grammys.

Canadian: Nickelback have won 12 Junos. Wait, what? That can't be right.

Super Bowl = Grey Cup

Tourist: I think the Patriots will win the Super Bowl this year.

Canadian: What's a Grey Cup? Is that something new on the Tim's menu?

Justin Bieber = Justin Bieber

Tourist: I think Justin Bieber sucks.

Canadian: I think Justin Bieber sucks.

Did You Know?

13% of roads lead to Avonlea.

Learn About Canadian Currency

Similar to the currencies in the United States, Australia, and New Zealand, the Canadian currency system uses loonies ($) and cents (¢). Visitors to Canada can exchange their precious, beautiful foreign bills for Canadian equivalents at every major airport or travel terminal, and at banks or currency-exchange storefronts in every major city. International credit and debit cards are widely accepted in Canada, though visitors should be forewarned that instead of inputting a PIN number on a keypad, cardholders are required to yell the names of hockey players who wore the numbers that make up their PIN. A purchase may sound something like this:

Cardholder: "I'd like to buy these winter tires, please. Here's my card. ALEXEI YASHIN, MARTIN STRAKA!"

Some visitors find it difficult to understand the symbols and icons on Canadian currency. Use this guide to help.

The Penny
The one-cent coin was discontinued in 2012 but is still legal tender. Known colloquially as the Timbit of Canadian currency, its only real purpose is for tossing off the CN Tower.

(PHOTO MISSING)

The Nickel
The smallest denomination in current circulation, the nickel's primary job is to protect the economy of Sudbury, Ontario. When dropped aggressively into a tip cup or the fare box of a city bus it can sometimes sound like a quarter.

The Dime
The dime is worth more than the nickel but it's smaller, as if that makes any sense.

The Quarter
The smallest denomination that you shouldn't be ashamed to use in a real transaction. Four quarters equal one Canadian dollar or one American quarter.

The Half Loonie

This is just two quarters. How did this end up here?

The Loonie

Named after a bird that, like the Canadian dollar, is often underwater.

The Double-Double

Introduced in 1997, the double-double replaced the paper $2 bill and is almost exclusively used to purchase extra-large Tim Hortons coffees.

Provincial Sales Taxes in Canada

All transactions in Canada are federally taxed at a rate of 8%, in addition to provincial taxes that vary from province to province:

- **British Columbia:** 7% sales tax, most of which goes towards paying for anti-depressants prescribed to the soggy populace
- **Alberta:** No sales tax at all, but sick and injured Albertans are left to fend for themselves in the unforgiving prairie
- **Saskatchewan:** 5% sales tax, although consumers wearing Roughriders merchandise are entitled to a 2% reduction
- **Manitoba:** 0% sales tax on most purchases; 100% sales tax on Slurpees purchased at the 7-Eleven
- **Ontario:** 8% sales tax, although secretly most other provinces' sales tax revenues go to Ontario as well
- **Quebec:** 9.975% sales tax, because Quebec makes everything more complicated than it needs to be
- **New Brunswick:** Those who have sworn an oath to protect the lighthouse must also pledge 25% of their crop yields to the gods of the tides
- **PEI:** 100% tax on leaving the island
- **Nova Scotia:** You get this round, I'll get the next
- **Newfoundland:** 5% provincial sales tax (harmonized with federal tax), which must be remitted half an hour before every purchase

1873 Prince Edward Island discovers bountiful brown plants underground

Visit Every CFL Stadium

BC Place, Vancouver

Home Team: BC Lions
Capacity: 54,500
Unique Feature: Each seat has cupholder and yoga mat holder
Trademark Snack: Foot-long Nanaimo bar
Fun Fact: Before the retractable roof was installed in 2011, the stadium had a fabric roof supported by nothing but air pressure and the always rising cost of Vancouver real estate

McMahon Stadium, Calgary

Home Team: Calgary Stampeders
Capacity: 35,400, one horse
Unique Feature: Flotation device under seats in case of Bow River flooding
Trademark Snack: An entire raw cowboy hat (if you finish it before halftime, it's free)
Fun Fact: Before every game, entire crowd passionately sings beautiful a capella version of "Sweet City Woman" by the Stampeders

Commonwealth Stadium, Edmonton

Home Team: Edmonton Eskimos [*Editor's Note:* Really? "Eskimos"?]
Capacity: 56,302
Unique Feature: Constructed entirely out of ice blocks; rebuilt every year after spring melt
Trademark Snack: A full-sized football helmet full of piping hot bison chili
Fun Fact: In 2003, hosted the NHL's first outdoor Edmonton Oilers loss

Mosaic Stadium at Taylor Field, Regina

Home Team: Saskatchewan Roughriders
Capacity: 33,427
Unique Feature: Used for alfalfa storage during the off-season
Trademark Snack: A loose handful of wild blueberries
Fun Fact: Only CFL stadium with a playing surface of wild prairie grass

Investors Group Field, Winnipeg

Home Team: Winnipeg Blue Bombers
Capacity: 33,500
Unique Feature: Men's bathrooms from old Canad Inns Stadium were painstakingly disassembled and reconstructed at IG Field to preserve the authentic "urinal cake smell"
Trademark Snack: Nine beers
Fun Fact: Many fans purchase tickets with the full knowledge that the stadium is located outdoors and in Winnipeg, Manitoba

1874 Quebec becomes angry

16

Tim Hortons Field, Hamilton

Home Team: Hamilton Tiger Cats
Capacity: 24,000 total hosers
Unique Feature: Entire upper rim of stadium
can be rolled up
Trademark Snack: Slightly burnt Tim
Hortons grilled panini
Fun Fact: After every victory, cars belonging
to fans of opposing team are melted down
and turned into steel girders

BMO Field, Toronto

Home Team: Toronto Argonauts
Capacity: Unknown; has never been full
Unique Feature: Because the Argos were
kicked out of the Rogers Centre, BMO Field
is technically zoned as a homeless shelter
Trademark Snack: Argonutella-filled
doughnut
Fun Fact: A pamphlet titled "Rules of CFL
Football" is placed on every seat before
each game

TD Place Stadium, Ottawa

Home Team: Ottawa Redblacks
Capacity: 24,000
Unique Feature: Instead of toilet paper,
washrooms are stocked with tax dollars
from western Canada

Trademark Snack: Tasteless bowl of trail mix
Fun Fact: After complaints by homeowners
in the nearby Glebe neighbourhood, all
cheering louder than a "dull murmur" has
been banned

Percival Molson Memorial Stadium, Montreal

Home Team: Montreal Alouettes
Capacity: 25,012
Unique Feature: Only stadium in the league
with a dedicated LARPing section
Trademark Snack: A single fist-sized cheese
curd
Fun Fact: Constructed in 1914, the stadium
has been able to drink legally in Quebec
since 1932

Did You Know?

Saskatchewan's most popular TV show is
CFL Gags.

Go Shopping

Canadians be shopping! Canadians list "shopping" as their third favourite pastime (being cruelly demanding of teenagers during the World Juniors and writing letters to the CBC insisting that *Road to Avonlea* be returned to television are numbers one and two, respectively). The history of retail in Canada begins with the Hudson's Bay Company. As early as the 17th century, HBC employed a network of brave trappers and talented craftspeople who laboured tirelessly to provide the future residents of Vancouver and Toronto with rustic interior accents and $400 blankets. Over time, these remote trading posts grew into a chain of department stores.

By the time of Confederation, when cities were growing in the East and homesteaders had conquered the wide-open prairie, Timothy Eaton saw an opportunity to bring his department store into homes from coast to coast. Offering everything from farm instruments to brutally restrictive corsets, the Eaton's catalogue quickly became a household staple. For nearly 100 years it was Canada's number one source of retail goods and toilet paper. The catalogue's place in Canadian culture was cemented with the publication of Roch Carrier's 1979 horror story *The Hockey Sweater*, about a young Montreal Canadiens fan's disturbing discovery inside a package ordered from the T. Eaton Company.

Although department stores have faded from the Canadian landscape, another big retailer remains ubiquitous. Canadian Tire operates close to 500 stores in Canada, and every year more than 90% of Canadians are disappointed to find that the snowblower on sale in the flyer is out of stock. The number one employer of sullen teenagers in the country, Canadian Tire is such an important part of the economy that it actually prints its own currency, passports, and marriage certificates. Unique to the organization is the Canadian Tire smell, a scent specific to this franchise and consistent from Dartmouth to Tofino. Government scientists have recently analyzed the smell (*see fig. 1*).

Significantly, nearly 20% of Canadian shopping doesn't take place in Canada. When the dollar is strong, long lines of Canadian cars cross the border to visit the outlet malls that occupy the northern fringe of the United States. In fact, nearly 40% of all Canadian lies are told to border guards

1875 First wedding registered at Hudson's Bay Company

fig. 1

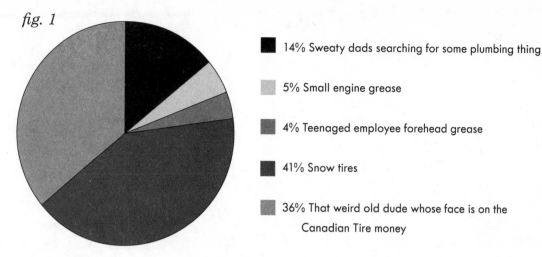

■ 14% Sweaty dads searching for some plumbing thing

▨ 5% Small engine grease

▨ 4% Teenaged employee forehead grease

■ 41% Snow tires

▨ 36% That weird old dude whose face is on the Canadian Tire money

who ask, "Did you make any purchases today?" This practice has a significant effect on the economies of both nations, draining loonies from Canada's prosperous southern cities and injecting them into America's weird, terrifying northern cities. When the Canadian dollar is weaker, the flow of commerce reverses and Canadian stores become 20% louder and ruder as Americans scavenge them for great deals.

One of the most notable American incursions into the Canadian retail landscape took place in 2013 when Minnesota-based Target acquired more than 100 Zellers stores and Zeddy costumes. With great fanfare, the first Canadian Target stores opened and excited customers flooded through the doors, only to find the remnants of a forgotten empire. Due to poor logistical planning, Target failed to plan any logistics, leading to empty shelves and furious deal-seekers. Today the stores

remain barren but Canadians remain hopeful for the return of the one true Zeddy.

Since 1999, Canadian spending on the Internet has increased dramatically; the average Canadian now makes more than 30 annual trips to Canada Post because they won't leave the damn package on the doorstep even though it's like a $9 HDMI cable for god's sake. It should be no surprise that Canadians love online shopping, since it sure beats chipping ice off your windshield and finding a place to park at the Bayshore Shopping Centre in Nepean, Ontario. And as consumers shift to online retailers, traditional "brick and mortar" stores are closing nationwide, significantly eroding the natural habitat of the suburban Canadian tween. However, like snails finding a new shell, Laser Quests and Halloween costume pop-up stores are taking over the empty spaces.

Visit New Brunswick

New Brunswick is one of the most beautiful and friendly places in the world, and yet it is shrouded in mystery. Magnetic Hill, the Ghost Ship of Chaleur, and the Moncton Murder Monolith are but a handful of the unexplainable phenomena found within its borders. Be sure to check those out, if you dare.

The province was discovered by Becki Ne'erbrun, an intrepid explorer cast out from her native lands far beyond the distant and foggy horizons. As the first woman in a long history of Ne'erbruns, she was commonly referred to as a foreign savage, but in reality she was just from Alberta. The Ne'erbrun family ruled for hundreds of years, until their house's power was eradicated by their bannermen, House Irving.

New Brunswick is primarily a lighthouse-based economy. As Ne'erbrun famously said,

She who controls the lighthouses controls the sea. She who controls the sea controls the land. She who controls the land controls the lighthouses.

True to this day, all local commerce is governed by those whom the lighthouse deems worthy of illumination. All shipments must be made at night, and must be accompanied by at least five sworn swords of the Brun Order.

New Brunswick's economy was significantly shaken by the lighthousing crisis of 2008. The devaluation of lighthouse-related securities, coupled with the realization of how boring fishing is, brought the markets to a standstill. The value of the New Brunswick dollar (the doubloonie) is so low compared to the Canadian dollar that local politicians have tried to establish a tax haven for foreign billionaires. This has only exacerbated the situation, eventually leading to the Second Frederictese War of 2014.

New Brunswick's magnificence knows no bounds, with untouched coastlines, ancient embattlements, and monuments to their founder's greatness. The Ne'erbrun Tower of Madness in Saint John draws nearly 10,000 tourists a year, all leaving with a newfound respect for the beauty of battle. Other must-sees include the Confederation Bridge, the Tidal Bore of Moncton, and the River of Betrayal.

However you choose to spend your time in New Brunswick, it's sure to be memorable. You may even want to move there! Just be careful, as all applicants for citizenship must pass a gruelling written exam and, of course, the Ne'erbrun Wartime Rituals. Good luck!

Complete the Five Feats of Ne'erbrun

90% of tourists in New Brunswick attempt the Five Feats of Ne'erbrun, near-mythical deeds said to be accomplished by the province's fearless leader of a time long gone. 0% of these tourists complete them.

Feat Number 1: Ascend the Forgotten Stairs

The stairs leading up to Saint John's city hall look like everyday stairs, but they hold a secret. A forgotten secret. It's said that there were once 100 steps up to the ancestral home of Ne'erbrun herself. Now there are a meagre six, but only to the untrained eye. Those who believe in the path of Ne'erbrun shall themselves ascend to greatness. The unworthy will merely ascend to the parking permit office.

Feat Number 2: Construct the Lighthouse de Triomphe

It is well known that the first thing Ne'erbrun did upon arrival in New Brunswick was build a lighthouse, staking her claim to the land. It stood 40 ships tall and was made entirely of elephant remains. Tourists to the lighthouse are encouraged to build their own little replica out of Popsicle sticks. No one has survived this feat.

Feat Number 3: Bathe in Your Enemies' Blood

Modern-day tourists can't partake in this feat for obvious reasons (Canada has no enemies), which is why many New Brunswick restaurants offer "Enemy's Blood" chicken wings. As the savoury sauce collects in the corners of your mouth, reflect on your foes and how they've wronged you. Bask in the knowledge that they can never hurt you or your countrymen again. Moist towelettes are strictly forbidden.

Feat Number 4: Tame the Wild Dogs of Bangor

A remnant from the Maine invasions long ago, these American attack dogs now exist only in stone form, serving as a monument on the Maine–New Brunswick border. The fierce totems inspire fear in all who lay eyes upon them, and if you can meet their gaze in battle, you don't have to pay duty.

Feat Number 5: Skate the Rideau Canal

No, it's not in New Brunswick and it's not much of a feat, but it's just something nice to do!

1876 First time the word "soaker" is used to describe a wet sock

Hike the Bruce Trail

Stretching nearly 900 megametres across southern and central Ontario's rugged wilderness, the Bruce Trail is one of the best places in Canada to experience bug bites. Every year, thousands of hikers take to the trail in an effort to make their kids do something, anything, other than sit at that goddamn computer all day, but only a hardy few successfully complete its entire length.

Starting beside a parking lot on the outskirts of Niagara Falls, Ontario (the Niagara Falls, New York, of Canada), the trail cuts a path along the stunning Niagara Escarpment, a world apart from the armpits of St. Catharines and Hamilton that it'll pass along the way. Beyond the Golden Horseshoe the trail veers north from the "affordable" family communities a two-hour drive from Toronto and up into the Central Ontario Wilderness (COW). As you go by the small town of Wiarton, say hello to Wiarton Willie, the famous local groundhog who can accurately predict the remaining weeks of winter, as well as how long till your beer is Cold Certified, and the length of a Stanley Cup drought. Finally, the trail follows the coast of the Bruce Peninsula, a rocky finger of the Canadian Shield that points across Lake Huron towards north-western Ontario like somebody answering the question "Where are the snowmobiles?" By hiking from a suburban parking lot to the rugged, unspoiled edge of the remote wilderness, it will be just like experiencing Canadian history in reverse.

It takes approximately 30 days, or the entire time that the Barenaked Ladies were cool in the United States, to traverse the Bruce Trail end to end. The record for fastest completion is currently 13 days, 10 hours, 51 minutes, or roughly the duration of one Avril Lavigne marriage.

Although the route is clearly marked and well maintained, hikers should take precautions against the usual dangers of the Canadian wilderness: poisonous plants, animal bites, soakers. Most hikers begin their treks during the warmer summer months, but the trail can also be completed during the winter—an experience only mildly more uncomfortable than the average wait for a Canadian city bus in February. Bring an extra pair of Vancouver 2010 mittens to be safe.

According to tradition, hikers who complete the entire trail are required to legally change their first name to Bruce, so the next time you meet a Canadian with that name, be sure to give them a slap on the back and say, "You had a pretty good walk there, eh bud?" Legend has it that every few years, all the Bruces meet at the trail to quietly walk and discuss their Bruce agenda. Want to join this secretive cabal? Take a hike!

Find Out Which Canadian Music You Should Listen To

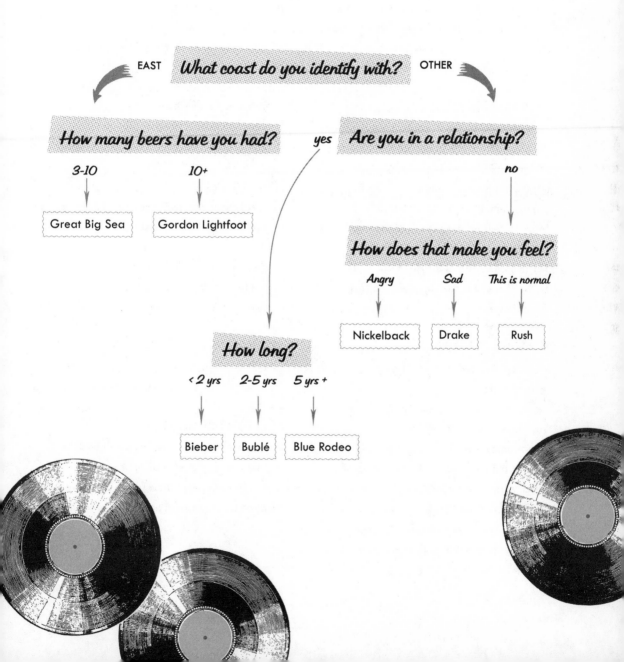

EAST ← *What coast do you identify with?* → OTHER

How many beers have you had?

3-10 → Great Big Sea

10+ → Gordon Lightfoot

yes

Are you in a relationship?

no

How does that make you feel?

Angry → Nickelback

Sad → Drake

This is normal → Rush

How long?

< 2 yrs → Bieber

2-5 yrs → Bublé

5 yrs + → Blue Rodeo

Score a Canadian Hat Trick

Canadian hockey fans are famous for throwing their hats on the ice whenever a player scores three goals in a single game. We estimate that more than 80% of free hats distributed in two-fours will eventually be sucked up into a Zamboni. Hat tricks are about more than just goals, though. Canadians also celebrate the "Gordie Howe Hat Trick," whereby a single player scores a goal, notches an assist, and gets into a fight. How many of these other Canadian hat tricks can you cross off your list?

CHAD KROEGER HAT TRICK
☐ Sell a million records, win a Juno, get a divorce

MIKE DUFFY HAT TRICK
☐ Buy a house, buy a cottage, cash a cheque from your buddy Steve

JOHN A. MACDONALD HAT TRICK
☐ Have a drink, then another, then just one more

MANITOBA HAT TRICK
☐ Get a bug bite, get frostbite, survive a bear bite

SIDNEY CROSBY HAT TRICK
☐ Win a Stanley Cup, an Olympic Gold, and a free doughnut in Roll Up the Rim

MIKE MYERS HAT TRICK
☐ Make a *Wayne's World* movie, make an *Austin Powers* movie, ruin your legacy with *The Love Guru*

EDMONTON OILERS HAT TRICK
☐ Win the draft lottery, win the draft lottery again, win the draft lottery again

NOVA SCOTIA HAT TRICK
☐ Get in your first fist fight, catch your first fish, get in your first fish fight

STEPHEN HARPER HAT TRICK
☐ Banish climate science, banish the press, banish modern hairstyles

JUSTIN TRUDEAU HAT TRICK
☐ Get a tattoo, hold a yoga pose for 45 minutes, elbow a woman in the boob

CANADIAN TIRE HAT TRICK
☐ Find an employee, ask an employee for help, get accurate directions to the product you were looking for (has never been accomplished)

DRAKE HAT TRICK

☐ Become a successful child actor, turn into the world's biggest rapper, turn into a meme

FRANK D'ANGELO HAT TRICK

☐ Bankrupt a beer company, bankrupt a movie production company, bankrupt

JUSTIN BIEBER HAT TRICK

☐ Become a YouTube sensation, pee in a bucket, get mistaken for Ellen DeGeneres

CANADIAN CLASSIC ROCK RADIO HAT TRICK

☐ Begin the day with a friendly voice, take care of business, go for a soda

Did You Know?

Gordie Howe is the only National Hockey League player never to record a "Gordie Howe Hat Trick."

Take a Domestic Flight

Before the invention of the airplane, few Canadians ever set foot in a neighbouring province, let alone a neighbouring time zone. Travelling great distances meant spending many uncomfortable hours waiting for an unreliable steam locomotive before being crammed into an overloaded train car. Today, Canadians who wish to visit other parts of the country enjoy long hours waiting for an unreliable airline before being crammed into an overloaded airplane. The future is now!

Canadian travellers enjoy the freedom to choose from over one (two) national airlines. Air Canada and WestJet serve communities large and small, connecting Canadians through a shared hatred of both. A handful of regional carriers offer service to more distant communities, with exorbitant rates for residents whose only other means of getting in or out involve holding on to a floating log and hoping for the best.

Air Canada

Founded in 1937, Air Canada operates the largest fleet, maintains the most routes, and generates the most misery. In addition to its main line, it operates the regional carrier Air Canada Jazz ("It's about the flights they don't offer, man!") and the budget-oriented Air Canada Rouge (notable for their cabin-crew uniforms styled after Men's Rights activists).

WestJet

WestJet is the "funny" airline. Their cabin crew is trained to lighten the mood with gentle jokes and mid-flight tickle fights. Initially a low-cost alternative focused on western routes, WestJet now offers passengers the opportunity to be disappointed across the country. Owned entirely by the employees, you can take comfort in the fact that the guy who let your underwear fall out of your suitcase and blow across the tarmac is basically the CEO.

Travel Tips

Air travel within Canada is much like air travel anywhere in the world, with a few significant exceptions. Pre-flight safety instructions can be ignored in both official languages, and federal law requires that half of all in-flight entertainment be completely unwatchable garbage. In addition to the

1878 John A. Macdonald wins a drinking contest and becomes prime minister for a second time

in-flight magazine, every seatback is stocked with the most recent Canadian Tire catalogue, and your chances of being seated next to a former Kid in the Hall are substantially higher than on a flight anywhere else in the world.

Due to the considerable distances between many Canadian cities, flights within the country are often punishingly long and dull. We suggest passing the time by gazing out the window at the lonely vastness of the northern hinterland and contemplating your own mortality, or playing Courteous Birds on your smartphone.

Flying out West? Don't forget to solemnly shake your seatmate's hand after safely passing over the peaks of the Rocky Mountains, as per polite tradition. Landing in the Maritimes? Remember to exclaim, "I doubted that this heretical metal bird could traverse the sacred skies, but it has safely deposited us back on the welcoming ground, just as the old lighthouse keeper predicted!" as soon as the plane's wheels touch down—you'll get strange looks if you don't.

Until humankind devises a more efficient way to conquer great distances, Canadians will be forced to depend on their domestic airlines to help them reach destinations as familiar as Prince Rupert, BC, or as exotic as Prince George, BC. So sit back, buckle up, and enjoy your complimentary handful of domestic produce!

Top Air Canada Complaints

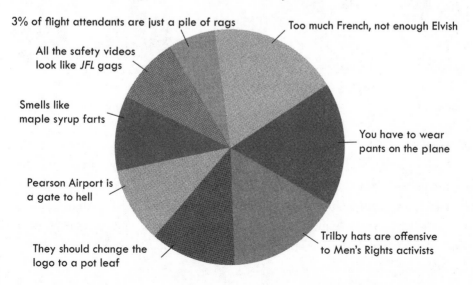

- 3% of flight attendants are just a pile of rags
- All the safety videos look like *JFL* gags
- Smells like maple syrup farts
- Pearson Airport is a gate to hell
- They should change the logo to a pot leaf
- Too much French, not enough Elvish
- You have to wear pants on the plane
- Trilby hats are offensive to Men's Rights activists

Pass the Citizenship Test

- Are you prepared to kill a close family member in order to survive the winter?

- What is the most valuable commodity in Canada, according to Stephen Harper?
  - ☐ Crude oil   ☐ Sweater vests   ☐ Winnipeg Jets   ☐ Regular jets

- Which of the following condiments are illegal to put on poutine?
  - ☐ Ketchup   ☐ Catsup   ☐ Dijon   ☐ Crude oil

- The campaign trains for two prime ministers leave their stations at the same time. Stephen Harper's train leaves Calgary at 10:00 a.m. Mountain Time. Justin Trudeau's train leaves Montreal at 8:30 a.m. Eastern Time. How long does it take for one of Harper's weird comments about "barbaric cultural practices" to ruin his chances for re-election?

- Describe "Canadian Tire smell" using nothing but hand gestures.

- Which Barenaked Lady is the bad one? (circle the bad one)

- What's the legal age for infants to begin smoking in Quebec?

- Rank these obsolete industries in order of highest unemployment rate:
  - ☐ Cod fisher
  - ☐ Oil worker
  - ☐ Auto assembly worker
  - ☐ Victorian whale murderer

- Do you love Marineland? y/n

- Identify these shapes:
  Saskatchewan
  A standard CFL field
  Burton Cummings's keyboard
  SkyDome jumbotron

- Number of dogs Don Cherry has named "Blue"?

- Hey, can you help me jump my car? It's in the parking lot. Thanks dude.

- Which of the following is *not* a real Canadian cultural award?
  ☐ Juno ☐ Gemini ☐ Genie ☐ Thickie

- How far away does somebody have to be before you are not required to hold the door open for them?
  ☐ 10 metres ☐ 25 metres ☐ 1 megametre ☐ Over the horizon

- How many extra *u*'s are in the Canadian alphabet?

- What does "K.D." mean?
  ☐ Canadian country singer-songwriter
  ☐ Inexpensive and delicious cheesy pasta treat
  ☐ "Keep Drinking!"
  ☐ All of the above

- Skill-testing question:
  <# of Dion Quintuplets> x <Lindros's Jersey #> + <Alcohol % of Labatt Blue > x <The Best Rock'Em Sock'Em> =

Text Like a Canadian

Canada is a vast country, with enormous expanses of empty space separating most people from one another. At any given moment, fewer than a dozen Canadians are within earshot of another person. To conquer these lonely distances, Canadians have long relied on telecommunications technologies to connect. The telephone, smartphone, and bananaphone were all invented by Canadians as a means to thank neighbours for clearing their driveways. As Canada's baby boomers are slowly left to perish on ice floes to make room for millennials, however, the emoji has overtaken the spoken word as Canada's most popular means of communication.

Most Popular Canadian Emojis

Bat Flip
The Littlest Hobo
French-Speaking Pineapple
Drake Crying
Pumpkin with a Crude Oilers Logo Carved into It
Potato That Looks Like a Butt (PEI only)
Rod Brind'Amour's Face
Gainer the Gopher
Pot of Kraft Dinner
Praise Hands (mittens)
Dead Raccoon
Poutine
Laura Secord Chocolate Bust
JFL Booger Mascot

Read the Tim Hortons Wi-Fi Terms and Conditions

PLEASE READ CAREFULLY. THESE TERMS AND CONDITIONS IMPOSE OBLIGATIONS AND RESTRICTIONS UPON YOUR USE OF OUR FREE WI-FI.

General

These "Terms and Conditions" between you and Tim Hortons set out duties and responsibilities associated with use of the Service. For the purpose of these Terms and Conditions, "you" means you and any person you authorize to use your device while you are in the bathroom. If you do not wish to be bound by these Terms and Conditions, you may not access or use the Service and you will instead be bound to use your expensive and unreliable data plan. Tim Hortons may modify these Terms and Conditions at any time without your consent or authorization, including modification or termination of the Service, or the addition of a web filter that replaces all jpegs with a picture of a slightly burnt grilled panini.

Acceptable Use Policy

You shall not use or allow others to use the Service if such use:

- Prevents other patrons from enjoying their low-grade coffee and poorly sliced bagels;
- Encourages the fact-checking of the group of slightly racist old men who linger in the dining area from 7 a.m. to noon every weekday;
- Includes searching SaskJeeves for the terms "I found a hair in my chili" or "This steak sandwich tastes like sawdust";
- Involves the sharing of photographs of Tim Hortons employees wearing mandatory company cowboy hats;
- Disparages the career or moustache of Sidney Crosby, including but not limited to fantasy hockey trash talk, the creation or promotion of offensive memes, and the deliberate misspelling of his name to perpetuate the stereotype that he's a crybaby.

Performance Levels

Tim Hortons does not guarantee the performance of the Wi-Fi Service, drive-through Service, or bathroom cleanliness of any location. You understand that the Service may be subject to network management in order to ensure that all users receive the same consistently terrible experience.

User Information

Your messages or Internet use may be subject to interception and review. Tim Hortons reserves the right to analyze such information to determine customer tolerance of lukewarm coffee, burnt coffee, and the maximum amount of time the average person is willing to wait in line for coffee. Please be advised that "liking" Starbucks on Facebook is grounds for termination of your access to our Wi-Fi network.

Miscellaneous

In no event shall Tim Hortons be liable for any failure to comply with these Terms and Conditions if such failure results from any condition or event beyond the reasonable control of Tim Hortons, including but not limited to kitchen fire, organized raccoon insurgency, employee revolt, disgusting washroom conditions, a snake on the loose, hockey riots (team loses), hockey riots (team wins), any natural disasters or acts of Gord, or malicious hacking perpetuated by those weirdos from Coffee Time.

1879 First case of food poisoning at the Canadian National Exhibition in Toronto

Visit Quebec

Quebec is known as "La Belle Province" because, much like Belle in *Beauty and the Beast*, it's trapped with a disgusting monster it would like to run away from. Quebec truly is a distinct society, separated from Canada by a unique culture, language, and the knowledge that every $5 bill you handle there has almost certainly been in a stripper's G-string at some point.

Visitors are often enchanted by the province's quaint towns, lively festivals, and ceaseless pranking. Pranks, known locally as "gags," are an important part of Quebec's culture; fake police officers outnumber real officers by 2:1, and nearly every trip to the store results in some kind of frightening pratfall. These pranks are so popular that the province recently introduced a new tourism slogan: "Quebec: We're Ready to Gag!"

When Quebecers aren't being assaulted by a fake construction worker, they're usually enjoying some of life's other simple pleasures. Quebecers consume more wine, cheese, and Pepsi than any other province, and they have contributed some important culinary creations to the nation's dinner tables and junior hockey arena concession stands. Long before hipsters made it a gourmet treat, poutine was a staple of Québécois cuisine. In fact, the story of Quebec's history is told in every plate of poutine: take some people from France (cheese), add a bunch of the Irish (potatoes), and then over-power them with a generous dollop of the English (gravy).

While the Catholic Church remains an important cultural institution in Quebec, its influence has steadily diminished since the Quiet Revolution of the 1960s. During this time, intense social and political changes displaced the Church from daily life and replaced it with Roch Voisine. Today, Quebec is a modern, secular province and the world's leading producer of devil stick jugglers.

Quebec's modern history has been marked by two contentious referen-dums on the topic of secession. In 1980 and again in 1995, Quebecers went to the polls to decide whether the province would separate from the rest of Canada. The votes were close, but in both cases the people of Quebec chose to step back from the brink and instead focus on gradually wearing down the rest of Canada's nationalist resolve with a steady stream of Céline Dion singles and temperamental hockey goalies.

In so many ways, Quebec is a nation within a nation, a cultural crossroads mixing Europe's Old World charm and eastern Ontario's aggressive love of grease and cheese. Enjoy your time in this beautiful province because, as they say in Quebec, *bienvenue au carnaval!*

Quebec Equivalents

Despite all their differences, English and French Canada have much in common. We've collected a list of famous English Canadian things and their Quebec equivalents.

Things	English Canada	Quebec
Obsolete sports relic	Don Cherry	Olympic Stadium
Thing of nightmares	Polkaroo	Bonhomme
Day of celebration and public urination	Canada Day	Fête de la Saint-Jean-Baptiste
Bordertown/butthole of the universe	Windsor	Gatineau
"I'm so proud of my daughter, she's a _____"	Neurosurgeon	Circus contortionist
Guilty pleasure	Carly Rae Jepsen	3 a.m. poutine
Beloved institution that everybody wants to bring back	*Are You Afraid of the Dark?*	Quebec Nordiques
Sexiest resident	Justin Trudeau	Justin Trudeau
Frenemy	Quebec	English Canada

1881 Canadian Pacific Railway is incorporated, one half-hour late

Learn About Quebec's Famous Battles

Canadians may be known as a peaceful breed, but the history of Quebec is dotted with conflicts both large and small. While it may come as no surprise that the province has a long history of picking fights (71% of babies born in Quebec are named after UFC fighters), you may not know about some of these notable clashes in Quebec's early and recent history.

Plaines d'Abraham

In 1759, on the hills high above Quebec City, the armies of Britain and France faced off and fought a bloody battle over the most controversial issue of the era: whose language should be on Canada's cereal boxes. The battle ended in a draw, and to this day every package of *flacons du mais* has an English side and a French side.

1976 Olympic Bidding Process

In order to beat out the other cities vying for the 1976 summer games, Jean Drapeau, the then-mayor of Montreal, personally started dozens of dumpster fires in Los Angeles and Moscow. When the other cities were forced to drop out due to the persistent stench of burnt garbage, Drapeau proclaimed that Montreal's games would be "the cementiest Olympics ever!"

Hockey Riots (ongoing)

After an altercation with a linesman in 1965, Maurice Richard was penalized for the cheap shot heard 'round the world, igniting decades of ceaseless hockey riots that have ebbed and flowed across the province ever since. The ongoing conflict has caused over $70,000,000 in damage (the equivalent of 500 large beers at Le Forum Pepsi).

Combat des Clips

In a conflict that spilled over into English Canada via the national broadcaster MuchMusic, Commander Craig F. Halket bravely stood guard as the week's hottest clips were pitted against each other every Friday night.

Quebec's Secret Culture War

After being defeated twice at the polls, Quebec's separatist movement initiated a quiet campaign of cultural subterfuge in 1996, dispatching waves of amiable secret agents beyond Quebec's borders in an effort to embed the province's goofy culture across Canada and beyond. Céline Dion, Martin Brodeur, and the entire cast of Cirque du Soleil are just a few of the loyal soldiers who have served their province in *le projet zoot-alors*.

1882 The rodeo is invented in Alberta; clown employment skyrockets

Get to Know Gatineau!

Located across the river from Ottawa, Gatineau is Canada's capital of F-U-N (A-M-U-S-E-M-E-N-T, en Français). Combining Ottawa's sleepy administrative soul with a uniquely French-Canadian love of MMA fighting and choppy haircuts for middle-aged women, this overlooked community offers the best of Canada's two solitudes. No trip to the Outaouais is complete without a visit to Gatineau: the filthy jewel of western Quebec.

- Fourth largest community in Quebec, after Montreal, Quebec City, and the roving horde of hockey rioters
- 66% of the local economy is sales of Molson Ice to Ontario teenagers
- Annual fireworks festival and hot air balloon festival are Canada's biggest inevitable fiery disasters
- Summer residence of Bonhomme
- Birthplace of Canada's most famous Daniels (Lanois and Brière)

When visiting Gatineau, don't miss the chance to take a tour of a genuine Canadian federal building! Any Canadian who presents last year's CRA notice of assessment is eligible for a free tour of Place du Portage. How many of these only-in-Gatineau sights will you spot during your visit?

- Questions from the public being ignored in both official languages
- Government stationery used to make note admonishing coworkers for leaving dirty dishes in the office sink

- Waste
- Federal employee complaining about length of commute from Barrhaven
- Nepotism
- Job titles that are just a bunch of letters and numbers
- A man staring blankly into the middle distance, his spirit gradually crushed by the inanity of his daily routine
- General malaise

Considered "too French" by many in Ottawa and "too Ottawa" by the rest of Quebec, Gatineau is a place without much identity. Formerly known as Hull, the name was changed after Bobby Hull insulted one of the city's most beloved chip trucks. In an effort to boost tourism, the city is considering other name changes for the future, but the current frontrunner, "20% Off Hotel Stays Longer Than Two Days, Quebec," has failed to gain much support. Whatever it's called, we know you'll love your visit—as long as you get there before the flaming hot air balloon incident.

Have a Montreal Bachelor Party

Until the 1970s, Montreal was both the largest city in Canada and the beating economic heart of the nation, home to the headquarters of virtually every major Canadian business and bank. Fears that separatists would successfully push the province towards seceding from Confederation, however, sent most businesses fleeing to the dull, predictable safety of Toronto. Today, Montreal's once vital economy is a shadow of its former self, but there is one industry that Montreal continues to dominate: the Bachelor Party.

According to the most recent census of hungover men, the typical Montreal Bachelor Party plays out like this:

Before the Party   Craig starts a group email thread to get things organized. The guys don't see each other as much as they used to, but you've all stayed close through a hockey pool that Danny ruins for everybody every year. You can't wait to see the gang.

8:30 a.m.   Road trip! The boys take the car seats out of their minivans and collect the crew, plus the groom's dad, Vern. This is going to be awesome.

11:00 a.m.   Pit stop! It's time to load up on Tim Hortons pulled pork sandwiches and clog the toilets at the ONroute.

12:45 p.m.   You arrive at the hotel that Tim reserved online, L'auberge qui Sent Comme les Cigarettes et la Sueur, right in the heart of Montreal's Curd Packing District. There are four beds and twelve guys, so you claim a spot on the floor because NOBODY'S SLEEPING TONIGHT, BOYS.

1:15 p.m.   You load up on beer from the "dep" down the street. The beers are huge and cheap here, and you can buy them everywhere! It's so civilized, you think to yourself. The rest of Canada should be just like this.

1:45 p.m.   Back at the hotel, you crack the first beer of the afternoon and promise yourself that you won't check your work email on your phone for the rest of the day. This weekend is all about "Les Boys"!

2:00 p.m.   Vern is shirtless for some reason.

2:30 p.m.   You're already on your third beer so you remind yourself to stay hydrated. You'll have a water after this one, you think to yourself.

3:15 p.m.   Vern, still shirtless, is handing out beers and has created a ping-pong tournament bracket. He actually carried a ping-pong table up to the hotel room.

4:00 p.m.   Beer number five. You still haven't had any water because you're afraid of Vern bullying you. There's a pay-per-view movie called *Les Boys* on in the background.

1883 Rodeo clown union becomes most powerful political entity in Canada

5:00 p.m. Brent, the groom's weird work friend none of you have met before, is telling you about all the activities he's planned for the evening. You lie and tell him that you checked out all the links he sent out ahead of time.

5:45 p.m. Somehow, you win the ping-pong bracket. It's the most athletic thing you've ever accomplished in your life. You experience a sensation of intense pride and confidence.

6:30 p.m. The beers are hitting you pretty hard so you discreetly pour some water into an empty tall can when Vern's not looking. You take one last quick look at your work email, but that's it.

7:00 p.m. A bunch of pizza from Amelia's shows up at the hotel and you all dig in. Danny uses a spreadsheet app on his phone to let you know that everybody owes him $13.43 for the food.

7:30 p.m. Brent finally convinces everybody to put their coats on, and you take three Ubers to a brewpub he has researched carefully. It's all planned out, he tells you.

8:00 p.m. The brewpub doesn't have any record of Brent's reservation. It's packed. Brent starts to argue, but James steps in—he took French until Grade 12, he's got this.

8:15 p.m. That didn't work. You all wander down Rue St. Tiguidou looking for somewhere to drink. Every bar is overflowing with very loud millennials. You wonder if the French call them "Les millénaire" or something.

8:45 p.m. You find a quieter bar down a side street. There are a couple of empty tables and a lot of TVs playing UFC. You count four people with neck tattoos.

9:30 p.m. You realize that Andrew's been in the bathroom for a while. You look around and see that he's been cornered by two large dudes by the pool table. Vern jumps up and pulls him out of trouble, and you quietly thank god that there was an adult around to take control of the situation. You finish your drinks quickly and leave.

10:00 p.m. Back on Rue St. Malcommode, Mike is leading everybody to a place he knows from another Montreal bachelor party last year. He says that it's perfect for tonight: big, lots of beers on tap, cool music. You can see a long line from two blocks away, but he promises that it will be worth it.

10:30 p.m. The line has barely moved. Your buzz is quickly fading. You begin to answer a work email on your phone but shove it back in your pocket after Vern calls you "employee of the month." Danny is trying to convince you to trade Jamie Benn for Zac Rinaldo.

10:45 p.m. You're finally at the front of the line. The bouncer lifts the rope to let you in, but stops Andrew with an outstretched hand. "Shoes," he says. Andrew is wearing a pair of grass-stained Reeboks with frayed laces. Nick tries to intervene but the bouncer won't budge. Danny says that it's bullshit and the bouncer points out that his shoes are pretty crap too. Mike glances around nervously.

1884 Canada graduates from high school

37

11:00 p.m. $160 later, plus cover, you're all in the club. You realize that Mike has brought you to the Mike-est bar in Montreal: it's loud, there are lasers, and they're playing a Kylie Minogue remix. You join the line at the bar and wait to order a $12 beer.

11:15 p.m. Shaun hands you a shot, and then another one. You toast the groom and throw them both back.

11:30 p.m. This place isn't so bad.

11:45 p.m. Shaun hands you another shot. Vern takes a break from dancing with two girls for just long enough to tell you that they're McGill students. You text your wife and tell her that you love her.

12:00 a.m. The DJ drops a song you've never heard and the place goes nuts. Andrew tells you that he's going to fight the bouncer on the way out. You buy Craig a beer and tell him that he's always been your best friend.

12:15 a.m. Shaun hands you another shot; that guy is your best friend. You talk to a weird man in a leather jacket for 10 minutes before you realize he wants to sell you cocaine. Mike, your best friend, keeps yelling, "Isn't this place great?"

12:30 a.m. James doesn't look very good; he says he's going to go outside for some fresh air. You're worried about him—he's your best friend! You pay the $6 fee to withdraw more money from an ATM near the bathroom. Vern's shirtless again.

1:00 a.m. Andrew doesn't look good either; he says he's going to go outside and find James. Craig says that he just peed beside Carey Price in the bathroom. The lasers are making you dizzy.

1:30 a.m. Brent is trying to get everybody to leave; you were supposed to be at the rippers hours ago. Are strip clubs even open at this hour? You don't feel so good.

2:00 a.m. The strip club, Les Gentlemen's Choice, is still packed. Your entire body feels heavy; you miss your wife. James and Andrew didn't make it—they belong to the streets now. A girl is taking her clothes off and dancing to the *Just for Laughs* theme song. The room smells like Febreze.

2:30 a.m. You haven't touched your drink, but the server makes you order another. Things are blurry. You're beginning to think that the Gentleman's Choice would have been not to come here in the first place.

3:15 a.m. You feel like you're trapped inside a Cirque du Soleil fever dream. Nothing makes sense anymore. The passé composé conjugation for *aller* keeps repeating in your mind, over and over. The room goes dark.

11:15 a.m. You all wake up at the hotel. James made it back, but he has a neck tattoo. You find Andrew asleep on a bench across the street and he says that he partied with Carey Price all night. You discover a resignation letter addressed to your boss in your sent emails. At least you won the ping-pong tourney.

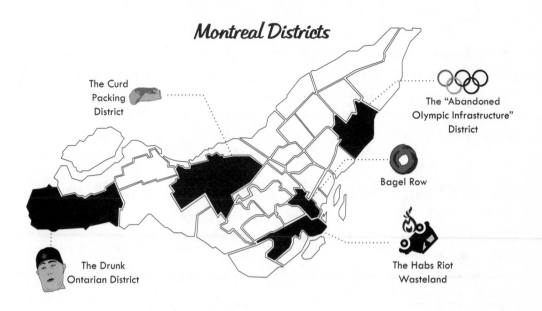

Montreal Districts

The Curd Packing District

The "Abandoned Olympic Infrastructure" District

Bagel Row

The Drunk Ontarian District

The Habs Riot Wasteland

Cure a Canadian Hangover

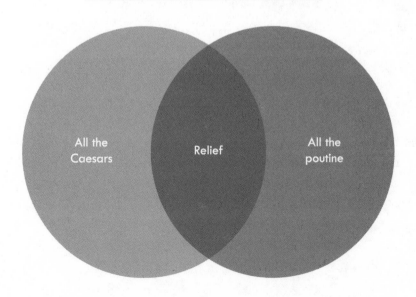

All the Caesars

Relief

All the poutine

Pick a Side: Leafs vs. Habs

Although Canada is currently home to seven terrible NHL teams, Canada's hockey history is still centred on the two oldest professional clubs in the nation: the Toronto Maple Leafs and the Montreal Canadiens. Understanding the similarities and differences between these two storied teams is crucial to understanding Canada itself.

Category	Maple Leafs	Canadiens
Number of years since last true moment of happiness	50	24
Logo	A leaf (looks great every autumn, falls off in the winter)	The letters C and H (abbreviation for "Centre Heiss")
Unique features of arena	Incorporates façade of old Canada Post facility in honour of a team that consistently mails it in	Fans in section 206 get one free Pepsi refill per period
Typical ticket holder	Middle manager for a corporate communication firm headquartered in Mississauga	Middle manager for an investment bank headquartered in Laval
Typical fan	Potato-shaped 43-year-old from St. Thomas, Ontario, named Brad	Chain-smoking 35-year-old from Laval named Antoine
Heroes	The winning ball in the 2016 draft lottery	Every former player, coach, Zamboni driver, and concession stand employee
Villains	Gary Bettman	Gary Bettman
Main rivals	Montreal Canadiens, Ottawa Senators, Fate	Toronto Maple Leafs, Boston Bruins, own fans
Odds of winning the Cup between when the author is writing this and when this book comes out	Zero	Zéro

Learn Quebec's Most-Used Phrases

Stats Canada surveyed the province of Quebec to discover the most-used questions and phrases uttered in "La Belle Province."

You never know when you might need directions to the closest washroom, so be sure to memorize these commonly used phrases on your next trip to French Canada:

Avez-vous des toilettes sans passager vomiting Ontariens adolescentes?

Do you have toilets unoccupied by vomiting teenaged Ontarians?

Quelle heure cette bibliothèque ne sert Montréal smoked meat sandwiches?

What time does this library serve Montreal smoked meat sandwiches?

Puis-je manger ce sandwich à viande fumée de Montréal sur le sol de cette bibliothèque?

May I eat this Montreal smoked meat sandwich on the floor of this library?

Je dois faire face à la crème pour mon bébé.

I need face cream for my baby.

La salle de bain dans ce musée de la poutine est un cauchemar.

The washroom in this poutine museum is a nightmare.

Désolé, je n'ai pas le temps de participer à un Juste pour Rire gag dès maintenant.

Sorry, I do not have time to participate in a *Just for Laughs* gag right now.

Cette baguette est remplie de raisins, et je voudrais remboursement.

This baguette is filled with raisins, and I would like a refund.

Mon engelures a empiré et je besoin d'un hôpital.

My frostbite has worsened, and I need a hospital.

S'il vous plaît aidez-moi je suivais un mime à un second emplacement et maintenant je suis le personnage central dans une esquisse Juste pour rire.

Please help me, I followed a mime to a second location and now I'm the central character in a *Just for Laughs* sketch.

Je suis respectueusement en désaccord avec votre opinion; Céline Dion est la plus grande chanteuse de notre generation.

I respectfully disagree with your opinion; Céline Dion is the greatest singer of our generation.

1885 Trans-Canada railway is completed with second-last spike (the last spike being Spike from *Degrassi*)

Learn *Tim Hortons* Etiquette

While the Canadian landscape varies widely from coast to coast, with rocky shore giving way to dense forest, broad prairie, and dramatic mountain ranges, one element of the national vista is identical everywhere: Canada's favourite coffee shop. According to our national doughnut and pastry census, there are 4,590 Tim Hortons locations across the country, which seems low but per year translates into roughly 390 million double-doubles, 290,000 burnt paninis, 13 honey crullers, orders repeated ad infinitum into the dinky drive-through speakers, and millions of older men sitting alone at a table, sipping on a coffee and staring out the window.

Tim Hortons has become essential to Canada's national identity through decades of being the only place to grab a coffee during your morning commute, annual pilgrimage to Grandma's house, or trip to the cottage you guilted your richer friends into letting you borrow for the August long weekend. We've put together a quiz to test your Tim Hortons etiquette and find out what kind of visitor to our national caffeine-and-carb chain you are.

1. You walk into an empty Tim's and see that all the tables are currently unoccupied. You:

a. Sit at a two-person table near the middle gathering of tables. You don't want to be in anyone's way.

b. Go for the large booth right near the rustic fireplace and casually drape your scarf, coat, and mittens all over the booth so nobody gets any ideas about sharing.

c. Tumble in, snarl at a child who looks alarmed, wander up to the counter, order a platter of grubs, berries, roots, and salmon, and growl upon being rebuffed.

2. The cashier informs you that they're out of Boston cream doughnuts, but if you'd like to wait there'll be more out of the oven in 10 minutes. How do you react?

a. "Oh, I am so sorry. Would it be easier if I ordered something else? Do you need any help in the kitchen?"

b. "How DARE you! What gives you the right? Where is the manager? I need to be compensated for this injustice to my person."

c. Stare blankly at the cashier and show your teeth before plopping onto the floor for a midday nap.

3. A large group of teens has been making a lot of noise for the better part of an hour, which is bothering everyone. You approach them and say:

a. "Excuse me, young people, would I be terribly out of line if I asked you to please keep down the noise? I'm so sorry to even ask. Really. I'm sorry. Actually, don't mind me. I should get going anyway. Have a great day. I'm going to get you guys some Timbits too. Be right back."

b. "If you terrors don't keep it down, I'll show you the meaning of an open-carry licence."

c. The teens take one look at you and run out, screaming.

4. It's World Juniors time and you happen to stop in during a game but notice the TV satellite has gone out. You:

a. Stream the game on your phone and invite people around the restaurant to watch with you. This is better than watching at home.

b. Loudly exclaim how Americans are actually better at hockey and continuously talk about the Miracle on Ice team and how the Blackhawks are a dynasty and cite the one American player on that team.

c. Gnaw on the corner of the TV.

5. You notice there's a bit of a mess by the garbage, with napkins tossed around and dishes piled up. You lend a hand by:

a. Gathering up all the trash and tossing it in the appropriate bins, stacking the dishes, and asking an employee if there's a mop you could borrow to clean up all the melted snow tracked in from boots.

b. Contributing to the mess by leaving all your trash at the table. That's why these people are paid minimum wage after all.

c. Trying to pick up a coffee mug with your paws, but break it and cut your paw. You howl in pain and scamper off into the woods to nurse your wounds in your den by the river.

Mostly As: You are a good Canadian, eh. Keep up the good work, buddy, and the next double-double is on us.

Mostly Bs: You're visiting from America, aren't you?

Mostly Cs: You are actually a polar bear! A carnivorous mammal found predominantly within the Arctic Circle that has been placed on the vulnerable species list due to climate change forcing habitat loss in the North. Visit the World Wildlife Foundation's website for more info on how you can help the beloved polar bear.

Hack the Tim Hortons "Secret Menu"

Looking at the posted menu is for suckers. Any Tim Hortons patron worth their dutchie knows about the secret Tim Hortons menu. However, if you're unfamiliar with the novelty of going into Tim's and ordering something gross that most people don't know about, we've compiled some of the most popular surprise items.

The Burnt Panini: A secret so well-known that it's actually become a staple. Order any panini off the menu and get it with a bun so dark it rivals Stephen Harper's heart.

The Toronto Maple Leafs Coffee Special: Hasn't been served in a cup since 1967.

Whopper Doughnut: Since being bought by Burger King, Tim's menu has become a little more diverse. Older generations will remember when it served just coffee and doughnuts and was a favourite spot for cops across the country. Yet, with American ownership, everything gets a little fatter. Walk up to the counter and whisper "Whopper doughnut." As you chow down on a doughnut sandwiched between two Whoppers you'll be asking yourself, "Was this really necessary?"

Rob Ford Sampler: A favourite of drunk university kids across the GTA. The Rob Ford Sampler gets you everything on the menu. Free if you're willing to swear in patois at the teenager working for minimum wage behind the counter!

The Justin Trudeau: A Timbit so sweet it'll give you a toothache.

Doughnut Gloryhole (NSFW): The name is the only description we can provide in print.

The Ben Mulroney: Order this and the kitchen staff will bring you a bucket of grease.

Café Moka Only: Much like the former member of Swollen Members, everything tastes better as a collaboration: enjoy steaming hot chocolate topped with coffee and thick whipped cream.

Other Helpful Tips

- Ask for an iced bagel: a cool and refreshing summer treat! (available one week per year)
- If you ask an employee to let you wear the drive-through headset, they have to give it to you
- Order chili by the "loose handful"
- Request that "no teens" touch your grilled panini
- Get a flavour shot of honey mustard in your iced capp
- Demand that they stop selling steak
- Ask them to play a different Shania Twain song
- Don't put Dad in a retirement home; Timmy's will let him sleep in a booth
- Tow a boat through the drive-through and all employees are required to salute you
- Dogs drink for free!

Avoid Dying in Ontario

Sure, Ontario is a beautiful place to visit and explore, but don't be fooled by the natural aura. Some of the province's best places to visit are also the most deadly. Each area highlighted on the map will most certainly end your life if you don't carefully avoid the indicated activities.

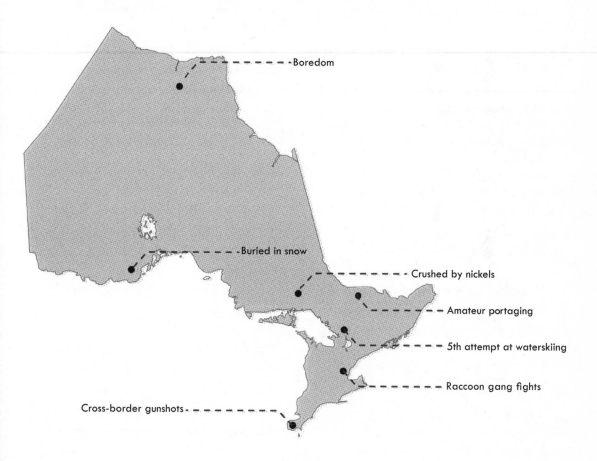

Boredom

Buried in snow

Crushed by nickels

Amateur portaging

5th attempt at waterskiing

Raccoon gang fights

Cross-border gunshots

1886 Great Vancouver Fire claims 80% of city, fuelled by burlap yoga pants

Go to TIFF

The Toronto International Film Festival is a two-week celebration of cinema that takes place each September. It has earned a reputation as the most influential fall film festival and the best way for a film to start garnering early Oscar buzz. It's also a great place to meet celebs and party on cool Toronto rooftop patios. 39% of Toronto residents tell everyone they know that they're 100% sure they just saw Scarlett Johansson at Chipotle.

Now entering its 42nd edition, the festival gets larger each year, culminating in hundreds of screenings, tons of A-list celebrities, and zero marriage proposals being accepted by Rachel McAdams.

FAQ About TIFF (TIFFAQ)

Where does the festival take place? The Toronto International Film Festival takes place in Toronto.

So it's like a film festival? The Toronto International Film Festival is a film festival.

Is the festival international? The Toronto International Film Festival is an international festival.

Can I watch the movies on Netflix instead? No.

If I run into Ryan Gosling at a bar will he fall in love with me? Probably not.

If I keep talking to Ryan Gosling against his security's wishes will I be banned from the festival? Probably.

Does this mean I should give up on my dreams of meeting Ryan Gosling and having him fall in love with me and marry me? Probably.

TIFF Tips (Tfps)

Do not approach the celebrities. They'll be scared off by your normality and won't know what to do.

Remember that film stars are people. One day they'll die too.

When celeb spotting, you'll spend 93% of your time standing in the hot sun waiting to see Brad Pitt for approximately six minutes. However, this return on investment is good if you're able to get a decent, not entirely blurry picture of him for Instagram.

When researching which movies you're going to buy tickets to, remember that the more pretentious the film summary, the better the movie.

If you're seeing a movie that was adapted from a book, make sure to loudly exclaim, "The book was way better," as you exit the theatre.

If you decide to ask a question during the Q&A after a film, make sure that either it's actually just a compliment for one of the actors or you spend so long talking about yourself and your experiences as an actor/writer/director that you forget to ask a question and they end the Q&A.

It is NOT funny to start your own lineup and tell people that it's the lineup to meet Ryan Reynolds. This bit does not get funnier as the line gets really long and girls start to cry when they figure it out.

Is That Famous Celebrity in Love with You?

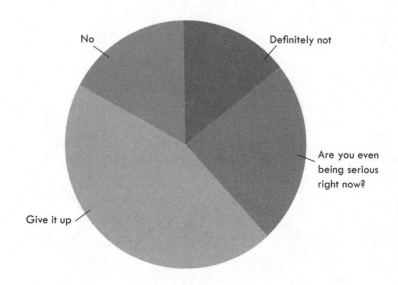

Visit an ONroute

Combining the convenience of a roadside rest stop with the ambiance of an airport food court, ONroute stations are Ontario's favourite place to settle for an Extreme Pita and overpay for gas. Located strategically along the 400-series highways, just far enough apart that 71% of Canadians can't hold it until the next one, Ontario's network of ONroute stations opened in 2010 and are the best place in the province to observe an exhausted dad from Orillia losing his patience. ONroute pit stops have become a mainstay of every road trip from Windsor to Ottawa and all points in between. And since many locations have both Starbucks and Tim Hortons franchises, it's possible to precisely determine your distance from Toronto by measuring the difference in length between the lineups.

Though the gas is expensive and the food overpriced, free perks abound: enter your email address, Twitter handle, Ashley Madison account name, or ICQ password to receive 10 minutes of complimentary Wi-Fi. Bring your damp tea towels along and dry them out using the state-of-the-art Dyson hand dryers! Wink at the local teen working the Burger King fryer and enjoy a loose handful of chicken fries when his manager isn't looking!

Next time you merge with highway traffic and set off towards your destination, tune your radio to the nearest Rush song and keep an eye out for the ONroute sign. While you're at it, watch out for these other common sights on Ontario's highway signs.

Ontario Highway Signage

Gas

Food & Drink

Nudist Retreat

Misbehaving Child Drop-Off

Text Stop

Sext Stop

Sweet Jump Ahead

Jazz Bistro

Birthplace of Avril Lavigne

Golf Course

Experience Ontario's Nature

Canada is renowned for its natural splendour, and Ontario is no exception. Any number of nature documentaries will show you the expansive forests, the great horned owls, or any of the other boring things that make Ontario beautiful. What no one is talking about are the wonders people see every day and don't even realize it. They're shrugged off as "concrete jungles" or "brutalist hellscapes," but those in the know simply call them the secret structures.*

Concrete can be found anywhere, but rarely is it triple reinforced to support bi-axial wind loads. Nature's gust has nothing on this pure foundation rooted unto the earth, barely seen but for those with access to underground parking. The next time you spot an 80-storey condominium with no green space or soundproofing, know that some of Ontario's beauty is hard at work, just below the surface.

Avid urban-sprawl enthusiasts will often seek out elusive beasts in the wilds of Ontario, known colloquially as cold rolled steel. Forged from the remnants of less beautiful provinces, the iron particles join together to form wondrous shapes, like sewer grates and traffic lights. Often coupled with their cousins aluminum siding and copper piping, these steel beams of light shine a path to the heavens, one load-bearing column at a time.

To fully appreciate the nature of Canada's most industrious sector, Ontario sightseers often keep a checklist of beautiful things to behold. How many have you seen?

☐ Neon Signs
☐ Red Light Cameras
☐ Combination Trash/Recycle Bins
☐ Shadows Cast on the Sidewalks of Condos Too Expensive to Even Gaze Upon
☐ Event Parking
☐ Record-Breaking Concrete Monoliths That Define a Nation

Concrete doesn't last forever. Even steel will fade with time. Ontario's infrastructure is slowly disappearing just as much as Ontario's natural beauty is. If we don't take time to stop and smell the structures once in a while, they may be replaced with newer and uglier ones.

---

* Sounds better when whispered.

1887 First log driver learns to step lightly

Have Fun on Lake Ontario

When Canada's brief summer finally arrives, Canadians are constantly looking for fun activities that will make them seem interesting when they tell their coworkers how they spent their weekend. If you're visiting the Greater Toronto Area, Stats Canada recommends a day on Lake Ontario! Take a look at all the fun activities the lake has to offer.

Lake Ontario: monster-free since '93!

Swimming

If your vaccinations are up to date, there's no better way to spend a hot summer day than swimming in Lake Ontario, nature's toughest swimming pool. However, beware of the fish that inhabit these waters. Toxic muck that has floated downstream from western New York and Hamilton has created a species of fish native to this lake. Scientists have yet to figure out how the Noxious Hammerhead is able to breathe on land but they're sure it's only 65% dangerous to human touch.

Also, beware of the beaver-tailed fish that inhabit these waters. As in a horror film, you never know when something's gonna pop out of the water and get you!

Boating

Boating on Lake Ontario is like trying to avoid icebergs while captaining the *Titanic*, except the icebergs are abandoned couches that refuse to sink and the passengers aren't poor Irish immigrants but this person you met on Tinder and only swiped right on because they had a lot of pictures with a boat and you wanted to go on a boat. 29% of Canadians will strike a *Titanic* pose within four minutes of being on a boat.

Beaches

Take in the fun of Hanlan's Point nude beach and play "Why is that old man staring at us?" Sometimes a drifter will wash up on shore but that's usually only about 2% of the time and they have to close the beach for only a couple of hours. Remember that any beach can be a nude beach if you put your mind to it.

Fun Facts!

Although Lake Ontario has the smallest surface area of all the Great Lakes, it's actually more about the motion of the ocean.

1888 Queen Victoria snubs invite to Canada, says, "Sorry, I just saw this message!" eight months later

In 1929, Baby Marie fell into Lake Ontario and when she was rescued they discovered she had grown an extra arm and a set of scales.

42% of boats on Lake Ontario are just showing off.

There are enough empty Molson cans in the lake to produce 323,000 wheelchairs.

In the Huron language, Ontario means "Lake of Shining Waters," but in 2017 it roughly translates into "Lake of Sludge and Old Car Parts."

The lake is the 14th largest in the world but currently holds the record for body of water with the largest amount of broken glass.

In 2005, they found a Ford Focus in the lake that had been there for seven years and it still worked fine after that.

72% of Canadians enjoy spending time outdoors in the summer because their mother has made them feel guilty about spending a nice day inside on the Internet.

Did You Know?

Honey, the average Canadian can't find the folding camp chairs. Have you seen them?

1889 Bad time to be a whale

Toronto is both Ontario's political capital and the nation's most populated city. "Canada's New York" has something unique to offer at every corner: the rats on Spadina, the hustle and bustle of Don Mills, the bagels of North Bathurst—the list goes on for this undisputed cultural hub of Canada and centre of the universe. However, as good as all these are, there is no other Toronto experience as authentic as being called a "[blank] Argos fan" or a "rat bastard" or a "shit-eating raccoon lover."

So our top recommendation for any visit to Toronto is to be demeaned in public. You won't have to spend too much time seeking this adventure—someone in Toronto yells expletives at someone else every 4.3 seconds.

Here are the top ways to be "told off" in Toronto.

1. CUT IN LINE (ANYWHERE)

Time is a very important commodity in Toronto—everyone, everywhere is busier than they have time for. Thus, if you're seen to be stealing someone's time, you'll be met with anger, curse words, and evil looks.

Common reaction: Silent expression of disbelief while looking up and down the line like "Can you believe this guy!?"

2. GO TOO SLOWLY DURING RUSH HOUR

Driving and traffic are the top annoyances of all Torontonians—and anything that exacerbates this horror will boil the demons to the surface of even the kindest Toronto public library volunteer-person. It's easy to elicit awful reactions from motorists: just get lost and drive slowly and unpredictably.

Common reaction: Aggressive horn blasts at first. Then as they overtake your vehicle, an awkward attempt to avoid all eye contact.

3. RIDE A BICYCLE

The tension between pedestrians, cyclists, and motorists is real. And in the Road Wars, cyclists are losing. These selfish environmentalists are loathed—even just mention a bike to a motorist and you'll get a 14-minute sigh of impatience. And God forbid you actually choose to get around on a bike: it'll put you in a lower class than the rats living under your favourite dumpling house.

Common reaction: A flippant hand gesture indicating that you don't belong on the road, or "How dare you use the extra foot-wide space—don't you know it's for me even though I never use it!?"

4. SAY SOMETHING THAT DOESN'T DIRECTLY SUPPORT DRAKE

Famous pop rapper and former child star Drake has been elected the People's King of Toronto. He holds a position amongst the gods. Any ill will towards the deity will be met with brimstone and fire. DO NOT explore this adventure.

Common reaction: Too explicit for this book.

If you're able to partake in this essential Toronto experience, you'll return from your vacation a little more jaded and a little more hip. You'll have the vulgar blood of the city flowing through your veins.

1890 Mississauga mayor Hazel McCallion is sworn in

See a Blue Jays Game

So you're in Toronto and you want to see Canada's team in action?

First of all, be prepared to pay mightily! Torontonians don't care about something until it's popular, and they love overpaying to feel like they're part of it all. Years ago, before they became the coolest thing to watch in the background during your tanning-and-drinking session at the SkyDome, pro ball players would show up at your house and beg you to come watch them play. You could be walking in the mere vicinity of the Dome and Ace the mascot would jump out of the bushes and thrust tickets into your hands. Now the only thing that costs more than getting drunk at a Blue Jays game is the actual tickets.

Make sure you know the players' names. There's nothing more embarrassing than not knowing who's on the team. Helpful hints: there's Bat Flip Guy, the dude who wears a mask and catches things, the cute one, that other guy, and, no, I know his name, it's on the tip of my tongue, just give me a second.

Instagram! Instagram! Instagram! How will people know you're at the hottest spot in Toronto if you're not taking dozens of selfies wearing a snapback you borrowed so that you can post a picture with the hashtag #lovethisteam? Make sure you stand up in the middle of play so that you can get the whole field and all the players in. People will start yelling at you but they're actually just yelling directions for your selfie. "Better lighting!" "Don't forget to smize!" "Not your best angle!"

Definitely have loud and inappropriate conversations while everyone's trying to watch the game. When fans around you cheer, make sure you pat them on the shoulder and say, "Please, sir. Do not interrupt us. Can't you see we're trying to have a conversation?" If you're having problems in your personal life, this is the venue in which to discuss them. The louder the better so that people can hear and offer their advice.

You'll want to leave early to beat the traffic on the way out. Don't forget to check TSN at some point to find out the score. If you know what happened in the game, you'll seem believable when you brag at work the next day about the game you were at.

Tips

- It's called the SkyDome. NEVER the Rogers Centre.
- You're allowed to bring in whatever food you want. Definitely bring that 12-foot party sub. You can share with your entire row.
- Don't be the drunk guy in your section spending the whole game trying to get the wave started.
- Don't be the drunk girl in your section spending the whole game trying to get on the jumbotron by flashing her boobs.
- Old men WILL shush you if you drink a little too much and start chanting Drake's name.

1891 John A. Macdonald dies; whisky surplus ensues

Rent an Apartment in Toronto

Over the last few decades, many of Canada's towns and smaller cities have experienced population declines as young people leave their hometowns in search of better job opportunities and faster Wi-Fi in Canada's larger cities. For those left behind, property is cheap and summer-snowmobile-storage options plentiful, but for those trying to make it in the big city, the cost of living can be crushing. The most recent census of millennial finances reveals that the average young Canadian in a big city spends more than half their income on rent, followed closely by food, transportation, and in-app purchases.

Finding housing can be a challenge. There's a shortage of apartments and lots of competition from other recent arrivals, making it difficult to find a place to call home. More and more people underneath the property ladder are having to settle for dank basement apartments, often marketed with euphemisms like "lower level," "cellar-style suite," or "damp cave chic."

To make things easier on Canada's laziest generation, fill out this standard rental application and send it to every slumlord on Craigslist.

Things Toronto Hipsters Liked Before They Were Cool

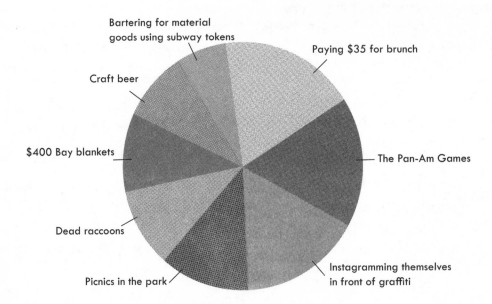

- Bartering for material goods using subway tokens
- Paying $35 for brunch
- Craft beer
- $400 Bay blankets
- The Pan-Am Games
- Dead raccoons
- Picnics in the park
- Instagramming themselves in front of graffiti

<table>
<tr><td>**Name**</td><td>**Date of Birth**</td></tr>
<tr><td>**Previous Address**</td><td>**Reason for Leaving Sarnia**</td></tr>
</table>

Payments Included

First Month_____

Last Month_____

Leap Month_____

References

Current Landlord:

Employer:

Your Parents:

Current Landlord's Parents:

High School Vice Principal:

Never have I ever?

Check all that apply:

☐ Hosted a house party

☐ Worn shoes in the house

☐ Started doing laundry after 9 p.m.

☐ Complained to the authorities about an apartment being used as an illegal rooming house

☐ Checked the batteries in a smoke detector

☐ Allowed a friend to sleep over

☐ Alerted the fire marshal about blocked exits, exposed wires, and piles of flammable material stacked haphazardly around the property

☐ Missed a rent payment

Visit Paris, Ontario

Tourists in Canada shouldn't miss the opportunity to visit Paris, Ontario (not to be confused with Paris, France, the "Paris, Ontario, of Europe"). Just off the picturesque Highway 403, nestled in the outskirts of Brantford, this quaint little town attracts millions from around the world.

Over 40% arrive accidentally, having intended to visit France's Paris. If you're one of these misguided travellers, make the best of your situation and try one of the following popular activities.

Art & Culture

Befitting a major centre of art and culture, Paris, Ontario, offers the opportunity to see spectacular masterpieces in person. Don't be surprised by long lines and big crowds, however, as other tourists strain to get close to national treasures like the vulgar graffiti behind the Canadian Tire or the ceramic mugs produced by Ms. Stasiyuk's middle school art class.

Food

A visit to Paris, Ontario, isn't complete without a meal at one of the town's famous restaurants. Parisians (residents of Paris, Ontario) enjoy cooking with rich, intense flavours from butter, lard, cheese, and fat. One of the best examples of traditional Paris, Ontario, cuisine can be found at the Pizza Pizza downtown. Call ahead to reserve your table!

Paris, Ontario, is also home to many legendary cafés where people from all walks of life gather to mingle, sip coffee, and debate the issues of the day. We recommend the historic Coffee Time.

Landmarks

Many universally recognizable landmarks dot the Paris, Ontario, skyline. Pack a picnic lunch and explore the town, crossing these buildings and monuments off your life's to-see list:

- L'arc de McDonald's
- The Eiffel Water Tower
- Château de Super 8
- Notre Dame Self-Storage

A visit to Ontario's famous "City of Streetlights" is an experience certain to live on in your memories, right along with the stink of cigarettes in your jacket.

1892 First women's hockey game played in Barrie, Ontario; both teams could probably beat the modern Leafs

Visit Dryden's Art Gallery

Art enthusiasts from around the world will tell you that their favourite tourist destination is Dryden, Ontario. Cleverly hidden in a community centre, the Art Gallery of Dryden is as shrouded in mystery as it is in misplaced gym mats. Who created the museum? When did it open? Even Dryden locals can't tell you when they first heard about it; they simply remember it as "just being there."

Origins aside, its patrons attend for the art itself. Home to such masterpieces as *Red Truck Against Blue Sky* and *The 14th Apostle*, the gallery/gymnasium floor is a feast for the senses. Patrons will find new additions almost every time they visit. Some say that the paintings change even while you're looking at them.

The Art Gallery of Dryden was made famous several years ago after an archaeologist discovered a Christian relic underneath one of the gym mats. Only then did the mysteries of the museum enter the public light. Since then, patrons have discerned cryptic riddles in stained glass windows, holographic paintings, and all sorts of curious clues unbefitting such a small-town tourist spot. When questioned, the museum's curator revealed himself as having been a descendant of the Knights Templar the entire time!

Visitors to Dryden all have wonderful things to say about the gallery, such as "Who knew that a gymnasium could be so full of intrigue!," "The albino man in the cloak was surprisingly friendly!," and "It's a shame so many had to die to cover up its secrets!"

If you care to experience the wonder that is the Art Gallery of Dryden, please note the following operating hours.

Days	Hours of Operation
Monday–Thursday	12:30–9:30
Friday	12:30–8:30 (Tome Club meets after close)
Saturday	Closed for gym cleaning
Sunday	Closed for secret catacomb cleaning

1893 Algonquin Park established in Ontario, renewing Canadians' love of pooping outdoors

Enjoy a Craft Beer from Every Province

Beer and Canadians go together like beer and stealing a Zamboni. For decades, Canada's taps flowed freely with Molson and Labatt's and little else. In recent years, however, the craft brewing craze has swept across the nation like a crisp and refreshing Alberta Clipper. Take your taste buds on a cross-Canada tour and enjoy these great brews!

Coast Mountain Brewing, Leaping Orca IPA
Vancouver, BC
Featuring pleasing notes of seaweed and salmon, this crisp, refreshing IPA is brewed with local Chinook hops and filtered through Lululemon yoga pants. Enjoy one at your next rained-out barbecue!

Blue and Gold Brewing Co., 88 Olympic Ale
Calgary, Alberta
Brewed with authentic Bow River floodwater, this beefy, full-bodied ale pairs beautifully with the lunch buffet at the Boudoir Rouge. With its 8.8% ABV, give the keys to your Ram 3500 to a friend.

Big Rectangle Brewing, Tommy the Commie Red Ale
Yorkton, Saskatchewan
Named after former Saskatchewan premier Tommy Douglas, the father of socialized healthcare, this alcohol-free red ale is produced using local grains and aged in hospital waiting rooms.

Gimli Glider Beer Company, New Iceland Blonde Lager
Gimli, Manitoba
With complex flavours evoking traditional Icelandic cuisine, this local specialty is the perfect complement to a boiled sheephead feast. Brewed with care by a team of stern and stoic grandmas in an old haunted warehouse. Grab a six-pack before your next Islendingadagurinn party!

Algoma Brewing and Snowmobile Parts Warehouse, Edmund Fitzgerald Porter
Sault Ste. Marie, Ontario
A Northern Ontario favourite brewed since 1971, this dark, rich, refreshing porter goes down easy. And since it's available only in cans, Edmund Fitzgerald also functions as a high-performance, two-cycle synthetic engine oil that improves efficiency and reduces wear.

1894 Original Stanley Cup awarded for the first time; fans immediately make their own out of tinfoil

Mineur Brasserie, Dernier Appel

Montreal, Quebec

A familiar sight in every university-adjacent depanneur, Dernier Appel is a drinkable lager at a reasonable price point. Available in Bro, Bruh, and Brahhh sizes, enjoy one on the patio or in your filthy off-campus apartment. Show your student ID for 10% off.

Ne'erbrun Mead, Traditional

Moncton, New Brunswick

Based on a traditional recipe from far beyond the misty horizon, this potent potable will fill your veins with the steely confidence of a grizzled lighthouse keeper. Keep away from open flames.

Green Apple Pilsner, Ales of Green Gables Brewing Co.

Summerside, PEI

Pouring with a clear straw colour and offering up the soft aromas of Granny Smith apples, this medium-bodied beer is a favourite of Japanese tourists and your aunt. Return the can for a 10-cent deposit or wait until you have 460 cans and receive one free trip across the Confederation Bridge.

Fake Fosters, Wrong Sydney Brewpub

Sydney, Nova Scotia

Inspired by the handful of total morons who show up every year in Sydney, Nova Scotia, thinking it's Sydney, Australia, this lousy Fosters knockoff provides little comfort to a wayward traveller expecting kangaroos but getting abandoned coal mines instead. Crisp and slightly tangy, it's better than nothing.

Soaking Dog IPA, Ballycater Brewing Co.

St. John's, Newfoundland

Brewed with melted iceberg water inside an old ship's boiler, Soaking Dog evokes the unmistakable scent of a damp Labrador retriever. Pair it with ham and the face of a fish, or enjoy it at room temperature on Regatta Day.

Did You Know?

76% of favours in Canada are done for free beer.

Dodge the Draft

Wars suck. 98% of all wars have resulted in at least one death. No one would want to take that chance, but sometimes there's no choice: your country will demand you fight for their political/financial advancement under the guise of "freedom" or "democracy."

Are you concerned that your nation will summon you to the front? Luckily for you, the Canadian government isn't into telling people what to do or who to fight (unless the Habs are playing the Leafs, amirite?). Canada is also a great place to defect—to hide in the woods, living out the rest of your days unshaven and wearing natural deodorant made of rock crystals.

Things to Do in Canada After You've Shamelessly Fled Your Civic Responsibilities

- Become an artisanal maple syrup distributor: Canada is full of maple trees just waiting for you to steal their sap, boil out everything but the sugar, and sell it by the Mason jar.

- Start a major outdoor-clothing brand centred on a beaver: Canadians will buy anything with a beaver on it.

- Join a folk band: nothing brings down the war machine quite like an acoustic guitar and soft, soothing vocals.

Whatever you choose to do, just be sure that you change your name, explain you've always been from Prescott, Ontario, and declare you'd rather die than see the New York Rangers win the Cup.

1895 We could say pretty much anything here

Cut Your Hair Like Wayne Gretzky

STEP ONE: Ask your dad if you can borrow his scissors.

STEP TWO: Practise cutting hedges in the backyard.

STEP THREE: Check your helmet for hair clearances.

STEP FOUR: Anticipate where the hair is going to be.

STEP FIVE: Get an assist from Messier.

STEP SIX: Cut away! Refer to the illustration below.

1896 Gold is discovered in Yukon; Prospector Chic takes off nationwide

Visit Alberta

Alberta offers a nearly endless bounty of snow-capped peaks, lush prairie meadows dotted with wildflowers, and a remote post-apocalyptic wasteland that will forever be a monument to humankind's self-destructive thirst for fossil fuels. Famous for its warm Western hospitality, don't be surprised if you never want to leave: many drunk Australians never do!

Human settlement in Alberta can be traced back to 10,000 BCE, when early Paleo-Indians migrated south down the leeward side of the Rocky Mountains in search of AAA-rated Alberta beef. European trappers poured into the region during the 17th century after wealthy Eastern city-dwellers demonstrated their willingness to pay good money for wearing part of a beaver on their head. Known then as "Rupert's Land," much of modern-day Alberta was controlled by the Hudson's Bay Company; the local currency was the "Hudson's Bay Rewards Point." It is believed that early residents would spend years accumulating these points, often letting them expire due to the complicated redemption process and lacklustre rewards.

After Confederation, an influx of homesteaders migrated across the Great Plains to work the fertile soil or start new lives as badass ranchers. These new settlers came from England, Ukraine, Germany, Norway, and innumerable other distant lands, but in their new home they would mix and blend into one beautiful and xenophobic people: the Hoser.

1897 First hitchhiker stranded in Wawa, Ontario

TruckNuts™ Sales vs. Number of Conservative MPs in House of Commons

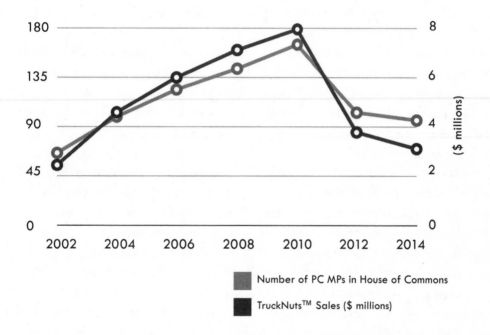

■ Number of PC MPs in House of Commons

■ TruckNuts™ Sales ($ millions)

Although the province's rough frontier history is a distant memory, reminders abound: Calgary's C-Train was only recently upgraded from a haywagon; Red Deer city police are equipped with lassoes instead of handcuffs; and rodeo clowns are everywhere.

Alberta is a beautiful destination year-round. Winter temperatures often drop below −40°C, but warm chinook winds can lift the mercury as high as an Oilers draft pick. Indeed, Albertans embrace the winter; the most recent census indicates that the average Albertan owns 2.2 snowmobiles and a pair of thermal underwear for each day of the week. The province truly comes to life in the summer, however, when the days grow long and the entire city of Calgary enjoys a week of cowboy cosplay called "The Stampede."

Albertans are fiercely proud of their province. While every Albertan is happy to fly the Canadian flag above their backyard or on the left shoulder of their Flames jersey, the average Albertan feels even more loyal to the baby blue Alberta flag and the symbols on it: soaring mountain peaks, golden fields, and a pair of TruckNuts™.

Travellers to Alberta will discover a province blessed by an abundance of natural resources, which makes it both a beautiful place to visit and a profitable place to excavate. Located in the northeastern corner, the oil sands project has powered much of the provincial economy for decades. In 2014, three of the five highest-paying jobs in Alberta were directly connected to the oil sands:

Geomechanical Engineer
- Roughneck
- Belt Buckle Shiner
- Crane & Rigging Supervisor
- Connor McDavid Replica Jersey Embroiderer

But ever since oil prices plunged as steeply as an out-of-control Jamaican bobsled team, many Albertans have seen their fortunes decline. Residents have lost as much as 50% of their annual income. Every six minutes, another Albertan misses a monthly payment on their full-sized diesel super-duty pickup truck. These proud prairie people have been reduced to brewing their own coffee at home instead of waiting in 45-minute drive-through lines at Tim Hortons.

It's never been more important that tourists spend their money here, so pack your favourite can of bear mace and Visit Alberta!

Who Could Better Manage the Edmonton Oilers?

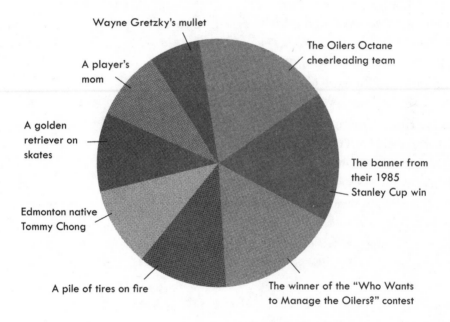

Wayne Gretzky's mullet

The Oilers Octane cheerleading team

A player's mom

A golden retriever on skates

The banner from their 1985 Stanley Cup win

Edmonton native Tommy Chong

A pile of tires on fire

The winner of the "Who Wants to Manage the Oilers?" contest

1899 Canadians fight in the Boer War; nobody knows what it is

Get an Alberta-Themed Tattoo

While tattoos can be found on Canadians from coast to coast, Albertans in particular love to decorate their bodies with local flair. No Regretzkis! Here are the 10 most common Alberta-specific tattoos.

10. The little rabbit from the Pils can
9. Ralph Klein's autograph
8. I (heart) Alberta Beef logo
7. The phrase "Save a horse ride a cowboy" with at least one typo
6. Harvey the Hound peeing on an Oilers logo
5. Full-body camouflage print
4. Sexy Preston Manning
3. Barbed wire (unironic)
2. Sexy Oil Derrick
1. A wild rose

Get to Know Calgary

As Alberta's largest city and home to many of its finest cultural institutions and filthy cowboy bars, Calgary is a destination not to be missed. Situated in the shadow of the majestic Rocky Mountains, its impressively modern downtown core is ringed by a haphazard, endless sprawl of suburban blight. The city's still riding high from its time in the spotlight as host of the 1988 Winter Olympics, and gets a bronze medal in hospitality.

Calgary's history and geography are tied to the mighty Bow River, which begins in the foothills of the Rockies and carries crushed cans of Pils all the way to the South Saskatchewan River. Named after Brian McGrattan's vicious elbow, it bends through downtown and gives Calgary its nickname, "The City of Bridges." Occasionally, springtime meltwater causes the swollen Bow to burst its banks, flooding the city with tepid brown sludge. The most recent major flooding took place in June 2013, causing catastrophic damage to many parts of the city, including the famous Stampede Grounds. The home of the Calgary Flames, the Saddledome, was also severely damaged, but it's been a decade since an Alberta-based NHL team played hockey in June, so no games were delayed.

Visitors to the city are greeted by a gigantic blue circle next to Calgary's international airport. The meaning of this massive piece of public art is unclear, but according to a recent survey of people milling around the baggage claim, the most popular guesses are shown in fig. 1.

Once a rough and dusty frontier town, Calgary has transformed itself into a modern metropolis. Fewer than 20% of all doors are those swingy saloon kind, and sales of player pianos have hit an all-time low.

Today's Calgarian is several generations removed from their ranch-hand ancestors, and although the Deerfoot Trail is gridlocked with full-sized pickup trucks every rush hour, most will be parked in front of office towers and not on job sites. However, every Friday and Saturday night, and for two weeks every July, the city puts on its finest white Smithbilt and celebrates the most hallowed Wild West tradition: binge drinking. At bars throughout the city, and literally everywhere else during the Stampede festival, you'll find rowdy Calgarians yelling and "maintaining a buzz." Line dancing, mechanical bull riding, and debating which Trudeau is the worse Trudeau continue to be popular leisure-time activities.

And yet there's more to Calgary than cowboy make-believe. In neighbourhoods like Inglewood and Kensington, young residents are transforming old boot stores into coffee shops and establishing liberal-minded outposts in the heart of Cow Town. Behind closed doors, brave hipsters are quietly practising time-honoured rites of passage, including drinking bad beer on purpose, hosting PWYC performance art shows, and pretending they know everybody at the party.

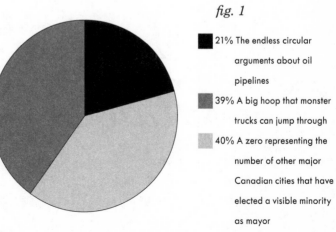

fig. 1

21% The endless circular arguments about oil pipelines

39% A big hoop that monster trucks can jump through

40% A zero representing the number of other major Canadian cities that have elected a visible minority as mayor

Attend the Calgary Stampede

The Calgary Stampede is the highlight of every Alberta summer. For two glorious weeks, the city grinds to a halt as everybody gathers on the Stampede Grounds to take in the spectacular events. Here's what you can expect to see.

The Parade
The official kickoff of every Stampede, the parade features more than 20,000 people, 4,000 horses, and every ass-kissing politician west of Saskatoon.

The Rodeo
The marquee event of Stampede, the rodeo boasts brave cowboys competing to see who can ride a bull until the beer buzz wears off.

The Chuckwagon Race
Basically just steampunk NASCAR.

Pickup-Truck Eating Contest
Watch as a man eats a whole truck, piece by shiny piece.

Best Hat
They're all good hats, but only one hat is the prettiest hat of them all. The winner receives another hat.

Hookey
No, not that sport. Stampede Hookey is a city-wide competition to come up with the most believable reasons for not coming in to work.

According to the most recent census of Alberta workplace absences, the most common Stampede-season excuses are as follows:

- Somebody stole my TruckNuts™
- My grandmother needed a ride to Stampede
- I was born a rodeo clown and this is my calling
- I am extremely sick today
- I am extremely drunk today
- I can't come to work because Stampede

MOST COMMON RASHES EXPERIENCED AT THE CALGARY STAMPEDE

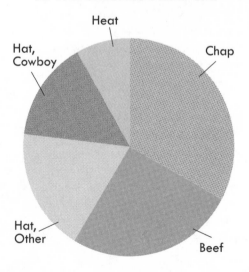

Fit In in Alberta

Alberta is a distinct province with its own unique culture and traditions. While the standard rules of Canadian etiquette apply, there are a few peculiarities for which every visitor should be prepared.

Visiting Homes

Don't be surprised if an Albertan invites you to visit their home; they're an exceptionally warm and hospitable people. It's customary to arrive with a small gift: we suggest a case of Pils.

As in many Canadian provinces, you're expected to take off your winter boots, snowmobile boots, or cowboy boots before you enter a home. Be sure to compliment your host's boot rack.

Food & Drink

Alberta is the birthplace of the Caesar cocktail, a drink combining local specialties like clam, Worcestershire sauce, and eight ounces of prime Alberta beef.

Visitors to Calgary shouldn't miss Ginger Beef, which is the name of a locally created Chinese food specialty and is incidentally also the name of the longest-serving dancer at the Boudoir Rouge.

However, Alberta's most important contribution to the Great Canadian Cookbook is the Prairie Oyster. Don't worry about what it is, you'll like it.

Tipping

It is customary to tip in Alberta. Bring a flashlight; it's going to be dark. Meet up by the old shed and then help each other climb over the fence. Walk quietly up to one of the sleeping cows and gently push the cow until it tips over. The number of cows you tip is up to you, but most people tip between 15% and 18% of the cows.

1900 Y1.9K bug affects adding machines

Visit the Drumheller Dinosaur Museum

Welcome to the audio tour of the Drumheller Dinosaur Museum, established in 1985 by a spooky archaeologist from Alberta.

Press Play on Track 1 to Begin Your Audio Tour
As you enter the gates of the museum, you'll notice you're actually walking through the jaws of a long-dead *Bronchiosaurus*. Our visitors often claim that it's easy to trip over the dull teeth.

Don't be alarmed by all the full sets of teeth you'll have to navigate throughout the tour. Nothing in the museum is explicitly designed to harm you, unless you count the fangs of hundreds of legendary monsters, sharpened through millennia of evolution.

Press Play on Track 2 to Continue
Our first exhibit is of fossils discovered in the province of Quebec, considered extremely rare in paleontological circles. Unearthed in 1994 by Jean-Louis Hardouin Michelin de Choisy, the collection includes the *Poutinadactyl*, the *Exposaur*, and the *Tyranglophone*. Some say that the ghost of Jean-Louis lives on in these fossils, and that their ghosts in turn live on to haunt other fossils.

Press Play on Track 3 to Continue
Moving along to the pride of Alberta, the *Albertasaurus*. Much larger than the *Edmontosaurus* and the Calgary River Monster, the *Albertasaurus* earned its name by being the hardest working dino in the country. Undeterred by naysayers, the *Albertasaurus* enacted an agenda that safeguarded the interests of his dinosaur friends and protected his land from foreign invaders.

Oh, did the lights just go out? Don't worry about that. It just happens sometimes.

1901 Queen Victoria dies; Canada sends an edible arrangement

Press Play on Track 4 to Continue

As you turn the corner, a swarm of animatronic raptors will jump out at you. Oh, did I warn you too late? Sorry. Maybe you should slow down a bit to maybe get your money's worth. That, and the dinosaurs can sense panic.

Press Play on Track 5 to Continue

Let's go underwater! Not all dinosaurs had legs, and it's best to remember that fact moving forward. Our fish tank contains fossils of some of the fastest sea creatures of the Jurassic period. Oh, it looks like the tank is leaking, slowly filling the museum with water. Now's the time to escape!

Press Play on Track 6 to Escape

As you swim up into the museum attic, don't be frightened by Alan the night janitor. His long white hair and soulless eyes are unnerving, but he's here to help. He'll direct you to Dino's Cove, where your ultimate goal shall be the Tail of the Last *Bronchiosaurus*. If Alan tries to tell you stories about previous guests' survival rate, don't listen. Alan doesn't know the truth.

Press Play on Track 7 as You Are Sliding Down the Spine of the Bronchiosaurus

Hopefully you've built up enough velocity sliding along the bones of an ancient beast to make it through the watery grave that was previously a museum. You'll soon find yourself violently exploding through the very teeth that once frightened you. What is dead may never die, and neither shall your lifelong membership to the Drumheller Dinosaur Museum.

Please Return Your Audio Tour Headset to the Nearest Molar

1902 First movie theatre in Canada opens in Vancouver; popcorn is already seven bucks

Get Health Insurance in Your Province or Territory

Province/Territory	Health Insurance Benefit
Nova Scotia	Up to 80% prescription donair coverage
Ontario	One backcountry hayride per year from an insurance-approved apple orchard
Alberta	One pair of cowboy boot orthotics every nine months
Yukon	100% coverage for a full-body tick exam each autumn
Quebec	Fully covered group therapy for all Bonhomme de Neige—related trauma
All of Canada	Free dental service for all puck-related injuries
Newfoundland and Labrador	75% flannel-dermis transplant surgery coverage
Manitoba	Free insulin shot for every litre of Slurpee consumed
Saskatchewan	Up to 80% emergency farmhand coverage
British Columbia	300 hours of gloom-related depression counselling per year
New Brunswick	Wounds sustained in battle cured free of charge at your local apothecary
Prince Edward Island	Two weeks off from work if you catch "Tater Fever"
Nunavut	Due to low supply of doctors, residents paid to cure themselves whenever possible
Northwest Territories	Bush-plane rides to hospitals now free of charge

Learn About Canadian Snowmobile Demographics

Recently, Stats Canada undertook a massive census of snowmobiles and their owners. The resulting data has produced some surprising discoveries about how Canadians relate to these "winter Jet Skis."

Canadians with Greater Than $100,000 Annual Household Income

Canadians in this demographic see snowmobiles as a means to dress in expensive winter gear and walk around their chalet village sipping imported hot chocolate. They are not concerned with useful technical features like Quick Adjustments or performance shocks.

Snowmobiles owned by these Canadians will spend 359 days a year in a garage piled under old volleyball nets, dog beds, and Christmas ornaments.

Canadians Living North of the 45th Parallel

For these residents, snowmobiles are more important than homes, education, and occasionally their third son, Phillip. Snowmobiles are more than a mode of transportation in the Canadian tundra; they're also entertainment, markers of social stature, a way to avoid getting a driver's licence, quick getaways after being caught with your neighbour's wife on a chilly afternoon, etc.

Snowmobiles are the second most important purchase a family will make in northern Canada, next to matching family Ski-Doo jackets.

This demographic accounts for 87% of all snowmobile purchases in Canada. In a short survey, nearly all Canadians from the North responded that they are not in favour of global warming because they would be so lost without their snowmobiles.

Canadians with Less Than $30,000 Annual Household Income

It may seem odd that this demographic would own any snowmobiles at all, given their $10,000 average price. However, more than 23% of all households in this income range own at least one—mostly because they're left to the family through a will.

The idea of a snowmobile as a "family heirloom" is a cornerstone of Canadians' survival as a people. Without these miraculous inventions, the Canadian economy could collapse. People wouldn't be able to make it to and from work, the grocery store, the liquor store, or anywhere else for that matter.

In fact, the population of Canada would decrease if it weren't for snowmobile ownership. The average Canadian snowmobile owner has approximately 12 more children than a non-owner does. Population growth would be unsustainable without snowmobiles.

1903 Suspicious inukshuk discovered in the Northwest Territories

Visit Manitoba

Beautiful, beautiful Manitoba. Once known for Indigenous trade routes and Icelandic cuisine, the state of modern Manitoba presents quite a different picture. Instead of the agricultural hub it once was, the province is now flooded with Alberta beef and whatever fish can be wrested away from the polar bears. A place defined by its lack of definition, its many lakes and abandoned mines mark the only shifts in elevation.

Still, the province is rife with culture, culminating in such events as the Fringe Festival, the Folk Festival, the Viking Festival, and the Anti-Viking Festival. Artists and Vikings alike flock to southern Manitoba in the summer months, filling the streets with impromptu dance numbers, bizarre street foods, and official Winnipeg Jets apparel.

The return of the Jets to Winnipeg has had a profound effect on the Manitoban economy. Most home games are sold out, so the scarcity of Jets tickets has turned them into a secondary currency in the greater Winnipeg area. One Winnipeg Jets ticket (WJT) can be traded for a Nintendo Wii, a good pair of boots, or in some cases, a small dog. The premier will let you rename Flin Flon for 10 WJT.

Manitoba sets itself apart from other provinces in many ways, including its provincially operated auto insurance program, known as the "Obamacare of insurance," or "Obamacar." The program is both loved and criticized, as it keeps prices down but allows poor drivers to retain their insurance even after several accidents. Another drawback is that in order to file a claim, you have to write a heartfelt apology to all those involved.

Capital city Winnipeg is statistically the coldest city in Canada, the flat plains and multiple lakes amplifying whatever cool winds the prairies can provide. Consequently, the intersection of Portage & Main is often considered the country's coldest intersection, and is home to Conservative Party of Manitoba headquarters.

Visitors to Manitoba can witness the full gamut of what Canada has to offer (except snowboarding). A haven for the outdoorsy, a wonderland for bear-attack lovers, and a playground for Aboriginal rights lawyers, Manitoba has it all, and so can you!

1904 Canada's official animal found murdered

Drive Safe in Manitoba

Manitoba offers a driving experience that differs from the rest of Canada's, with unusual road rules, controversial insurance laws, and poorly dressed Uber drivers.

Road rules include the Michigan Left, the Albertan Right, and the Ontarian Lane Change Without Signalling. Driving the pine-lined back roads of Manitoba, you'll notice that most of them don't have lane markings—they've been scraped away after years of salt and ice.

Access to rural areas actually improves over the winter, as Manitoba's many lakes become ice-road highways. This seasonal grid connects communities that otherwise lack easy access to major townships. Still, in the summer months these highways become problematic for fishermen, who have to avoid the traffic signals sticking out of the water.

When travelling to northern communities, be sure to avoid hitting polar bears with your car. The bears are attracted to the smooth contours of luxury vehicles, even at highway speeds. It is best to keep driving that old truck of yours so as not to excite the animals with a fancy pickup. (The number one cause of death for polar bears is the 2017 Ford F250 Eddie Bauer Edition.) And when parking your car overnight, remember to leave the doors unlocked so that polar bears can climb inside if they get too cold.

Like a handful of other provinces, Manitoba has a provincially run auto insurance program—a system that makes certain everyone is insured. But the cost of a Manitoba driver's licence depends on a Driver Safety Rating (DSR), a scale that ranges from +15 to −20. And if you can't maintain a safe driving record, you'll face some unique constraints (see the table below).

Overall, Manitoba is a safe place to drive, as long as you don't have to go north of Selkirk, work at a mine, or park on the street in Winnipeg.

DSR	Restrictions
+1 to +15	No restrictions; access to all Manitoban roads (except the road out)
0	Same as above, but cops will give you a lollipop as encouragement if they pull you over
−5 to −1	No access to roads that have more than seven children playing hockey on them
−15 to −5	Allowed only on Phil's Road, Bear Attack Boulevard, and Winnipegosistobanappalachitoba Road
−20 to −16	No access to roads located on the Canadian Shield

1905 Canada is quite pleased with its wheat production

Fix Climate Change

For anyone who's gone outside in the last 20 years, you may have noticed the latest passing craze: climate change. Do your snowmen lack longevity? Are the mountains on your beer can slightly less blue? No longer able to access Russia via land bridge? You may be a victim of climate change.

Previously known as "global warming," "climate change" better reflects the plight of Canadians. Outsiders may think "global warming" may do Canada some good, but in reality it can lead to a much colder environment as well. Just ask Manitoba. That place is crazy. Studies have shown that even the bears wear jackets. Yes, they're Winnipeg Jets jackets. Yes, with the old logo.

As things get hotter in some parts of the world (polar ice caps, George Clooney), things are getting colder in others (Hudson Bay, that minute between getting out of the shower and drying yourself). The jet stream, formed along the boundary of hot and cold weather patterns, has shifted wildly in the last decade: warm weather is happening farther north and cold weather farther south. This is known as a "polar vortex," or as Texans call it, "What's All This Canada Crap?"

or "The Devil Has Brought Snow and the Devil Will Be Made to Pay."

What's the source of these potentially disastrous goings-on? Some argue that the change in weather is natural—that it has nothing to do with the massive amounts of carbon humankind has blindly injected into the atmosphere, the precious barrier between us and the cold death of space. Others contend that there's no change at all, despite declining sales at their snowmobile dealership. Still others think the problem is animal farts.*

Whatever it is that's causing these global weather patterns, it's having a profound effect on the people of Canada. Climate scientists predict that within 10 years we'll start seeing errant icebergs in Vancouver Harbour, PEI will have been eliminated by a tsunami event, and the only beer available will be Labatt Ice.

The conditions of life in Canada will be so severe that residents will be forced to:

---

* *Editor's Note:* While collecting this data, the authors had to visit anti–climate change websites, forever ruining their targeted ads.

- Eat less meat (chickens found a way to fly away from Canada)
- Support the Roughriders (due to severe weather events, all CFL teams will be renamed the Roughriders)
- Cut open Bonhomme de Neige to use him for warmth (like a tauntaun in *The Empire Strikes Back*)
- Dip into the whale oil reserves (as established by Sir Wilfrid Laurier, Enemy of Whales)

What can Canadians do to combat or even reverse climate change? Experts suggest walking to work, taking shorter showers, and sharing pools with your neighbours. The more pessimistic experts say that our small efforts are futile, and that we should start building doomsday bunkers (not to be shared with neighbours). Stats Canada proposes something a bit more ambitious. Move to America.

Okay, hear us out. Americans could learn a lot about climate preparedness from their half-cousins to the north. As weather drops in the United States, Canadians can teach them how to make jackets out of foxes, how to hold a Timmy's without burning yourself, and how to pronounce the word "tuque."

And it's not like there won't be room for us. The entire population of Canada can easily fit in the Grand Canyon, creating the world's largest kitchen party.

The real change will come when Canada's environment reacts to the emigration of its people. The streets will turn into gardens, the animals will fertilize, the oil sands will remain oily. The CN Tower will be overrun with ivy, absorbing all the carbon that's been in the atmosphere since the 407 was built. Hockey rinks and Princess Autos will become carbon sinks and grottoes. Canada will teach the world to heal, and it will have nothing to do with politicians, scientists, or statisticians. We'll be saved by Canada itself.

1907 Canada loses a bet, has to shave Saskatchewan

Experience Car Trouble

Canada's roads can be beautiful, monotonous, and even deserted. But they're also dangerous. Car troubles are common, so here's a breakdown.

Province / Territory	Car Trouble	Root Cause	Solution	Tips
Quebec	T-boned some guy from Ontario	The guy ran a yellow	Guy had it coming	Further embrace your separatist roots
Ontario	T-boned by gravy train	Inefficient spending at a municipal level	Call a tow truck, do not expense it to the city	Call the mayor
Alberta	Head-on collision	Bull bars on hood of car did not effectively deter bull	Ride bull to nearest town	Tip the bull, but don't tip the bull
Saskatchewan	Car filled with grain	Could not properly navigate around grain silo	Drain the grain by rolling the windows down and doing sweet driving manoeuvres	Get up-to-date grain silo locations from the provincial website
British Columbia	Car has been grinded by a sick snowboard trick	Sick snowboarder	No solution, as you've been owned	Ask them to tag you in the Facebook video
Territories	Car filled with bears	Bears got cold	Buy a new car for the bears	For optimal bear comfort, get them a van
Manitoba	Veered into a snowbank trying to avoid a game of street hockey	Local teens	Grab your gear out of the trunk and offer to play net	You can retrieve your car after the August melt
Newfoundland & Labrador	Car is currently being repossessed	Failure to make sufficient car payments	Buy the repo man some Timmy's and he'll call it a day	Head west for gainful employment
PEI	Car has become beached	Accidentally driving off the edge of the province	High tide	Get a GPS that understands tiny provinces
Nova Scotia	Actually you're in a boat	Boats are often better than cars	Take a second boat back to your car	Try to clean the boat stink out of your clothes and car
New Brunswick	Car stabbed by Vikings fighting over land rights	One set of pirates claimed they were there first	Stab the strongest pirate to assert dominance/dominion over the land	Reap the land for benefits far greater than any automobile

Give a ZED Talk

Knowledge is power. The leaders of today and tomorrow are sharing their minds with the country through the power of ZED Talks. Do you think you have what it takes to educate Canada? What will you talk about? Allow us to make some suggestions:

- What Changing the Oil on Your Snowmobile Can Teach You About Being a Father
- Neil Peart: Drum Solos Inspired by Highways
- The Statistical Science Behind the Leafs' Miserable Failures
- How Farmers Will Shape the Future of the Bunz Trading Zone
- How Stephen Harper's Piano Playing Is Saving Lives
- Have We Reached Peak Tuque?
- How Google Glass Will Change Your Opinion of Don Cherry
- The Hidden Calories Behind Harvey's Pickles
- Why the National Anthem Has Ruined So Many Relationships
- Welcome to Inuit Internet
- The Surprising Demand for Whale Oil
- A New Kind of Poutine for a Post-Harper Economy
- A New Type of Tractor, Powered by an Old Type of Tractor
- How Gordon Lightfoot Influenced a Whole Generation of Senators
- Why the Beaver Tails of Tomorrow Are Already Eaten
- How Lloydminster Got Its Groove Back
- Why Canada Post Still Isn't Important

1908 Redheaded scamp captures the heart of nation

Spend a Day with the Queen

Part of every Canadian's birthright is a free trip to England to spend a day with the Queen. Many Canadians do not take advantage of this offer, as it is difficult to get a sub for rec hockey, but those who do make the trip are in for a royal treat.

Guests of her majesty have several options for accommodations, including Berkshire Castle, the Berkshireham Oldcastle, and Berkshirehamtrough Goldcastle. You will be delighted by any option you choose. All overnight stays come with a complimentary Queen Robe and Queen Soap. Ask Ben at the front desk about the soap.

Your day with the Queen begins by joining her and her various corgi mixes on a walk along the royal family's private river. Like all Brits, the dogs enjoy the affection of strangers but will never let you know it. The Queen, on the other hand, will regale you with colonial pleasantries. You'll start to feel your Canadian patriotism melt away as you eat breakfast on horseback.

Lunch is served in the courtyard, the dogs long since forgotten. You'll enjoy a royal egg salad sandwich made from the eggs of monarchical chickens who've dominated their poultry fiefdom. Royal juice boxes are available, but considered optional. Still atop your horse, you'll tour the Queen's private chambers where she sleeps modestly, having only three beds (shared with the corgis).

Tea time. Irreverent Cockney butlers bring you hot tea and crisps while the Queen admires your conversion skills, wearing the coldest of smirks. Her Project Assimilation accomplished, you'll be asked to leave just before a 10-course supper is served. Your British zeal has fully ripened by now and you'll be crippled by this sudden fall. Now you truly understand what it means to be a royal subject. You'll be directed to Her Majesty's Passport Office to begin becoming a British citizen and paying British taxes.

As you settle into your new life on the other side of the pond, you may find your thoughts drifting towards Canada and the life you've left behind. Try not to fight these feelings, as you will only bring about the scorn of the Queen. The Queen hath provided you with a new life, and she's let you keep the horse.

1909 Five-pin bowling invented in Toronto; doughy uncles rejoice

Get to Know Boomer

Residents of PEI have been put under a spell. It's not something in the water or in the potatoes; it's something in the airwaves. Kevin "Boomer" Gallant has become the most trusted weatherman on local television. His predictions, contrary to those of the heathens at the Weather Network, are treated as gospel. Boomer's appeal is so great that even his distant relatives are local celebrities. In fact, the most successful pick-up line in PEI is "Boomer's aunt is also my aunt," narrowly beating out "Hey, you kinda look like Anne of Green Gables."

Talk to the locals: Boomer's influence is noticeably pervasive. Ask a resident why they're wearing a Nor'wester (Boomer's own brand of raincoat) on the sunniest day in July; they'll respond simply, "Boomer said rain." Hours later, the clouds will roll in and drench the province. Well-prepared islanders smile. Boomer said rain.

In recent years, PEI has experienced more severe weather events than ever before. Some point to global climate change, but others know better.

"If only people would listen to Boomer more, we wouldn't have these terrible storms," says one resident. "If Boomer summoned rain, there's gonna be rain," says another.

The word "summon" comes up often. It evokes a sense of mysticism, and yet if there is a mystery to this Boomer, surely other Canadians would have heard of it by now. For their part, locals swear there's nothing mystical afoot, and that merely "We must obey the summoner's wishes, and buy his brand of luxury rain apparel."

Speaking directly to Boomer himself, some say, is a difficult task. Reaching his castle atop the summit of Junction Road Hill was a herculean feat. But Boomer is actually a thoughtful, well-spoken man who inspires trust in all those around him. We spoke for only a few moments. After I purchased a raincoat from him (he'd advised it would rain), I was left with an almost euphoric feeling.

Later on, as the rain poured down upon me, the bliss was multiplied. Sheltered in my ceremonial Nor'wester, I could only smile. Boomer said rain.

1910 First annual Terry Fox Hunt takes place in Manitoba

Discover Saskatchewan

With boundless fields of wheat and enough horizon for a lifetime of sky-gazing, Saskatchewan is truly Canada's top destination for wholesome family fun and adventure.

History

Until it became a province in 1905, Saskatchewan served as little more than an enormous pit stop for tired cross-country travellers. By 1910 the population had surged from 90,000 to 400,000. Settlers from Europe were offered acres of land for nearly zero cost, which holds the record for Canada's largest Boxing Day sale.

Geography

One of the only two landlocked provinces, Saskatchewan is often referred to as the "meat" of the Prairies, sandwiched as it is between Alberta and Manitoba. Its territory spans both the Canadian Shield and the Interior Plains, with lush boreal forest in the far north and wheat stretching over 88% of the land. Many residents have even taken to replacing grass lawns with miniature fields of wheat, making Saskatchewan the country's most sustainable province in the event of a gluten apocalypse.

Economy

For years Saskatchewan was known for having Canada's dullest export: grain handling. But since 2009, when *Corner Gas* aired its finale, the province's main export has been series DVDs and memorabilia. Sales of gift shop items like Brent keychains and Oliver Leroy mugs featuring the grumbling yet lovable old coot and his trademark quips are now a major part of Saskatchewan's economy. Exports have done exceptionally well in South Korea, Argentina, and the Czech Republic. In the Philippines, however, the show receives an R-18 rating owing to the suggestive nature of its name, which directly translates to "The Butt-Man's Gas Factory."

Holidays & Festivals

First Week of February: Winter Lentil Festival
95% of the country's lentils are grown in Saskatchewan, making Canada the world's top lentil exporter. Each year, Yorkton locals celebrate everyone's favourite flat legume. Festivities include a parade, the lentil recipe exchange, and of course the Little Miss Lentil crowning ceremony.

1911 Mary Pickford becomes first Canadian actor to move to L.A.

April 13: Corner Gas Day

Corner Gas Day commemorates the run of Saskatchewan's most popular show. All local channels broadcast its six seasons commercial-free. Although it's not a statutory holiday, gas stations remain closed for 24 hours.

May 29: Honey Bee Day

A radical holiday honouring Saskatchewan's favourite insect. The holiday was deemed "too menacing" for the general public and denied by the provincial legislature. Honey Bee Day is observed in an unknown location, by a bee extremist organization rumoured to dabble in the Swarming Arts.

August 3: Brent Butt Day

Brent Butt's birthday. Saskatchewanians honour the father of prairie-specific comedy by speaking entirely in *Corner Gas* quotes.

Daylight Savings Time Spring/Fall: Lloydminster Festival of Clocks

Tens of hundreds of "Clockers" gather to spend a weekend on the Alberta border in Lloydminster, the only city in Saskatchewan that participates in daylight savings time during both Spring Forward and Fall Back.

Residents & Customs

Many Flatlanders reside in the southern half of the province, having been drawn to its larger, more populous cities: Regina, Saskatoon, Moose Jaw, Moose Palm, East Salmon Arm, Swift Current, Rough Drift. Saskatchewan is known as Canada's friendliest province. Most locals will invite you to sleep on their spare couch. This is especially jarring for city slickers who are not accustomed to extreme acts of paying-it-forward and obsessive-compulsive kindness.

Cuisine

Most of Saskatchewan's comfort-food cuisine—rich dairy, fresh fish, endless lentils—retains a strong Ukrainian influence. Saskatoon berries are by far the province's favourite berry, used in dishes, sauces, jams, pies, fish topping, coyote bait, and various satanic rituals.

Saskatchewan truly is the capital of family fun, and they want to keep it that way. Did you know that all visitors to Saskatchewan are required to sign a "fun waiver," making it legally binding to have a good time there? As of this printing, over 8,000 boring visitors have been detained or heavily fined. So don't be a square; hit up the Sask!

1912 Maritime pawn shops flooded with pocket watches stolen from *Titanic* corpses

Visit the Saskatoon Wheat King

If you find yourself taking in a show or sporting event at the SaskTel Centre, be sure to pay a visit to the Wheat King, a larger-than-life blade of wheat that looms over the arena's south entrance. The statue—a literal interpretation of the Tragically Hip song—was erected in 1999 to commemorate the band's sold-out Saskatoon concert that year.

The SaskTel Centre hadn't just seen an opportunity to construct a legendary Canadian monument. Given the lack of other events in the city and the resulting overflow of non-ticket-holding teens and lookie-loos who'd heard something was "happening down at Sask Place," the Wheat King was also meant to create a photo opportunity for guests and thereby ease bottlenecking.

The structure was designed collectively by 12 Saskatoon-area elementary school classes who participated in the "Spruce Up Sask" contest, which called on local students to design a monument based on any Tragically Hip song. The first-place submission was a tie between all 12 classes, each of whom submitted the same design. The second- and third-place submissions were based on the songs "Locked in the Trunk of a Car" and "Nautical Disaster," but both were deemed "inappropriate and frightening" and were disqualified.

A month after the unveiling of the giant copper wheat blade, controversy struck again when it was stripped of its jewels and precious copper, leaving only its cold, unseeing eyes. Its replica was made from a less expensive metal, and is accompanied by a stern warning that metal looting will not be tolerated.

The monument stands two metres high, its weighty bronze core plated with gold. The devil is in the details, however: it looks out through a custom set of googly eyes, currently holding the record for the world's largest, and the crown atop its head is a replica of the crown worn by King George VI as an infant.

Statistically, the bronzed blade is Saskatoon's most well-liked glutinous structure, holding the record for the most Instagrammed wheat-related monument in Canada. It also has a social presence on Twitter; although no official page exists, the Wheat King parody account boasts an impressive 100k followers, tweeting daily facts about wheat in an aristocratic tone.

DID YOU KNOW? Every song title on the Tragically Hip's set list the evening of their concert on February 27, 1999, is engraved on a kernel of the Wheat King.

DO YOU BELIEVE IT? The Wheat King is the highest-ranking member of the Saskatchewan legislature. Tie votes are decided by shouting "Yea" and "Nay" directly at the monument and measuring which sound produces the loudest echo.

1913 Jefferson McClung Arthur Aerplayne named eighth prime minister

Match the Saskatchewan Resource with Its Use

Resource	Use
Alfalfa	Hot dog additive
ATV lube	Air travel M.D.
Buffalo hide	Fuel
Brent Butt	Garnish
Canola	Understudy chickpea
Cherry whisky	Non-car oil
Corner Gas Blu-ray	Jams and preserves
Lentil	Barbaric skin covering
Leslie Nielsen	Instagram filter
Moose cheek	Sturdy doorstop
Oil	Perfect for cocktails
Potash	Maintaining gluten levels
Swamp gas	Fertilizer
Black Swift Currant	Star of Corner Gas: The Movie (2014)

Visit the Fictional Birthplace of Canada's Favourite Redhead

Discover Prince Edward Island, red sand on a croissant-shaped land mass. Miles from the mainland, PEI is the moody mistress of the Atlantic. It's also a top destination for vacationers who prefer moist conditions in low- to medium-degree isolation.

History

Prince Edward Island's roots, like much of Canada's, lie in a bustling Indigenous population. In PEI's case, it was the Mi'kmaq who inhabited the land long before it was renamed Île Saint-Jean and claimed as a French colony in 1534. Down the line, the land was traded to Great Britain for a rather large bag of wigs. The province was eventually named Prince Edward Island after a brief period as St. John's Island, a loose translation of Île Saint-Jean.

Geography

The smallest province of Canada packs a powerful punch when it comes to lush greenery, panoramic views, and endless photo opportunities with lighthouses. The island is located north of the Nova Scotia peninsula, west of Cape Breton Island, and east of the elusive province of Ne'erbrun. PEI's natural landscape is highly protected by a number of laws, including the outlawing of chewing gum and the enforcing of cruelty-free brush clearing. Additionally, humans feeding any wild animals, such as ducks, must give them gluten-free grain products.

Economy

With PEI growing roughly one-third of Canada's potatoes, the scruffy ground apple is the top export, followed closely by the miniature straw hats produced for Anne of Green Gables dolls.

Holidays & Festivals

First Week of February Holiday
A holiday that marks the end of January's cruel reign. Locals typically take the week off and celebrate getting through the calendar's least favourite month. Avoid travel, as all shops, banks, and official/unofficial Anne of Green Gables tribute museums are closed for the duration.

1914 Thousands of young Canadians embark on exciting trip to Europe

April 29: Blue Jay Day

Blue Jay Day is mostly an exciting affair, but the last 5% of the day is disappointing, as unexpected visitors from Cleveland tend to ruin it.

June 8: Anne of Green Gables Day

Every year the remaining six townspeople and a dozen out-of-towners flock to Cavendish for Anne of Green Gables Day. Attendees gather in the parking lot at the Anne of Green Gables museum for freckle painting and old-timey fun. Participants love re-enacting the early 20th century, although each year 60% of them contract dysentery.

Winter [dates vary]: Great Potato Solstice

The Potato Solstice coincides with the Winter Solstice and is thus a mandatory farming celebration for all PEI residents, who prepare for the upcoming harvest by thoroughly tilling the soil. If you wish to partake, ask a local if they need help burying land apples. They'll know what you mean.

Residents & Customs

With a staggering 94% of the population made up of natural redheads, it is customary to berate blondes and brunettes in public. Many tourists bring a redhead wig to help them blend in. Anne of Green Gables doll–style wigs are available for purchase from all official/unofficial Anne of Green Gables tribute museums.

Cuisine

When you visit any Atlantic province, it is customary to take in the rich marine culture and eat it, too! According to PEI tradition, you not only choose but also catch and tackle your own lobster, luring it out of the ocean with nothing but a piece of red yarn tied around a hefty local russet potato. It's an interactive, tactical, and delicious activity for the whole family.

Notable Residents, Celebrities

- Anne of Green Gables
- Anne of Avonlea
- Mike Duffy (seasonal)

1915 Euro trip is not going well

Visit the Potato Museum

The world's largest, and possibly only, museum dedicated to the craft of growing and harvesting potatoes is located right in the community of O'Leary in the western part of Prince Edward Island. Although 36% of visitors claim to have wandered in by accident, the website boasts that "many" visitors come from all over to take a picture with the world's largest potato sculpture, and the Internet never lies so this must be true.

Founded, surely as a prank, in 1993, the museum flourished for years until PEI got its first dial-up Internet connection in 2014. The museum has not recovered from the distracting allure of modern technology and has since suffered from poor ticket sales. Nevertheless, the museum remains optimistic that attendance will once again jump when the PEI government makes the potato legal tender in 2018.

While you're never more than 30 minutes from a beach on PEI, you're also always within sight of the museum, as its potato sculpture remains the highest freestanding object on the entire island.

Museum Highlights

In 2015, the museum held a potato give-away to try to attract more visitors. Three people showed up, including one guy who ate raw potatoes like they were apples. This event was not repeated in 2016.

The museum experienced a 73% spike in attendance when they removed the "No Irish Allowed" signs from the front door after the 1997 release of the feature film *Titanic.*

Considered the "bad boy" of the potato world, scalloped potatoes have their own display in the museum. It's cordoned off by a velvet curtain and rope and is 18+ only.

A portion of the museum caught on fire in 1996, destroying the collection of potatoes that resemble Anne of Green Gables. The air smelled like French fries for weeks and islanders came from all over the province to savour the aroma.

The museum has a cafeteria that hosts different potato-themed nights. The most popular is Mashed Potatoes Monday, but 64% of Canadians remain convinced that their mom makes the best mashed potatoes in the world.

Surprisingly, only one wedding to a potato has taken place at the museum. The couple have been married for four years and are very happy together.

1916 Manitoba becomes most female-friendly province by allowing women to vote

Top Uses of Potatoes in PEI

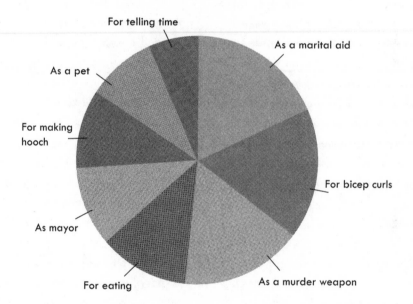

For telling time

As a marital aid

As a pet

For making hooch

For bicep curls

As mayor

For eating

As a murder weapon

1917 Canada grows chest hair at Vimy Ridge

Risk Hypothermia in the Canadian Territories

Consider visiting the Territories, nestled on top of Canada's more temperate provinces. The three enormous and partially livable ice formations—Yukon, the Northwest Territories, and that fresh-faced new kid on the iceblock, Nunavut—feature over two highways shared between them and offer sights and experiences unlike anything else south of 60° or this side of Hoth.

History

The Territories weren't always known as the World's Largest Ice Rink. In fact, it wasn't until Guinness World Records awarded them the title (and several other ice-related titles once GWR was told that the northern patch of land was not an extension of Alaska) that they earned their status as the planet's second most lifeless and inhospitable expanse of ice. Toronto's Air Canada Centre is number one.

Geography

The landscape of Yukon, the Northwest Territories, and Nunavut is actually much more than just ice and endless banks of snow. It's rumoured that Yukon is able to sustain a variety of spruce trees in some of Canada's most tepid temperatures, plunging well under freezing during much of the fall and winter and reaching comparatively tropical conditions in the summer. Most of the land is just ice, though.

Economy

Main exports include canisters of pure arctic air, unpasteurized penguin milk, and decorative whale soaps, available for sale in all gas stations and airport gift shops.

Holidays & Festivals

Spring Equinox Festival of Lights

Festivities are planned months in advance, with townspeople gathering in the square to witness the first sunrise of the season—a stunning display complemented by local Inuit throat singers who entertain crowds with traditional ballads about the miracles of spring. Jars are passed around to "trap" the light. Traditionally these jars were saved, but now they're sold as a novelty online.

Summer Solstice Festival of Grass

Although this celebrates the promise of grass poking through the ice and snow across the vast tundra, most people come for the six-hour Inuit throat singing competition. Similar to *Canadian Idol*, the festival showcases top Canadian talent, and competitors are judged on their harmony, costumes, and showmanship.

Fall Equinox Festival of Hidden Grass

Perhaps the most solemn of festivals, the Hidden Grass Festival mourns the end of summer and braces for the transition to endless darkness. As per tradition, local Inuit throat singers gather to perform popular covers of songs to shine some light on an otherwise dark observance.

Winter Solstice Festival of Friendship

During the harsh winter months, residents are encouraged to stay indoors and get to know their neighbours by engaging in a group cuddle. Most gatherings are small and held within tightly knit communities. It is customary to tune in to a live radio broadcast that counts down the top throat-singing hits of the year.

Residents & Customs

The Territories now have over 100,000 inhabitants combined, and are home to the country's highest concentration of Aboriginal peoples. Still, humans are outnumbered by sled dogs by a staggering 300%.

Given the high cost of importing everyday produce and luxury items alike into the Canadian tundra, it is customary to trade canned items, cases of water, and snowmobile parts. The going rate for an iPhone is nine cans of meat and a ride into town.

Cuisine

In traditional communities, it's not uncommon to eat "country food," usually consisting of meat caught and butchered on the tundra itself. However, the recent spike in veganism that accompanied the arrival of TV and Internet from the south has sparked the arrival of many new foods, including faux caribou, or "cariboux," and tofu beluga, or "tofuga."

Notable Residents, Celebrities

- Big Jeff, the guy who'll always help out when your truck gets stuck in the muskeg

- Adeline Tompkins, star of "Snowmobile Injury Lawyer" commercials

- Gramma, who will love you no matter how much you bring back from the hunt

- Yukon Billy, third-generation Yukonian and volunteer park ranger at Ivvavik National Park

- Charlie Crow, disc jockey and politician

1918 Spanish influenza spreads quickly across Canada due to opening doors for each other

Sample a few CanCon Favourites

Starters & Sides

Fryin' Adams
A side of classic hand-cut fries drowning in gravy.

Nickelbabyback Ribs
Succulent ribs simmered overnight in Hard Roque Café's signature BBQ sauce. Served with a side of trademark Chad Kroeger curly fries.

If I Had One Million Donairs
Be careful what you wish for! Our donair sauce is 85% cocaine!

Entrées

Belieberberry Encrusted Cod
Battered cod covered with a mixture of Belieberberries and panko, fried until golden brown, and served with rows of corn when available.

Our Lady Pizza
A former favourite of ours, this aging pizza comes with four toppings: self-important pepperoni, acoustic cheese, middle-of-the-road mushrooms, and a garnish of sour grapes.

Chris Sheppard's Pie
Cut and mixed from the finest seasonal vegetables, this baked dish will get you on the dance floor. Best enjoyed while using a fake British accent.

at the Hard Rocque Cafe

Beverages

Avril Taurine

The secret ingredient of energy drinks, now available in its purest form! Turns a man into a boi!

Kim Mitchell's Bottomless Soda

Had a rough day in cottage country? Might as well partake in our sugar-free pick-me-up, served lukewarm.

April Wine

Mostly flavourless, with a greasy aftertaste.

Sangria Twain

Enjoy a glass of seasonal frozen fruit in a sweet, earthy punch of orange, brandy, and red wine. Sure to impress you much.

Dessert

Draked Alaska

Finish with a slice of pure "6": layers of frozen ice cream encased in a gooey layer of meringue.

BranVan Muffins

Like the band Bran Van 3000, these guys won't stick around very long—in your bowels that is! Get things moving with the Roque's delicious bran and raisin muffins.

Tiramitsou

A large enough serving to satisfy any cowboy, this decadent treat is a rich and sensual experience that your dad remembers vividly from the late 80s.

A good time

The kind of time that Trooper is here for

Not a long time

Meet the Real Houseboatwives of Snout Harbour, NFLD

One of Canada's most unique contributions to the popular reality TV genre is the *Real Houseboatwives* series. If you find yourself in Deer Lake, Newfoundland, be sure to check out the houseboatwives of Snout Harbour, where guests are treated to a behind-the-scenes look at the lifestyles and flashy boathouses of the Rock's most-watched ladies.

Mary MacDonald

When Mary MacDonald isn't tending to her gigantic 2,400-square-foot houseboat, *Mama's B'y*, this houseboatwife can be spotted antiquing for upwards of six hours a day, feeding her uncontrollable compulsion for porcelain rabbits. It's no secret to the chatty houseboatwives of Snout Harbour, though Mary's troubling behaviour is completely unbeknownst to her husband Ronnie, a seasonal lobster fisherman who's at sea most of the year.

Emma McCarthy

She may be four foot nine, but Emma McCarthy is truly captain of the ship. In both her family life and as mother hen to her circle of friends, she's earned the nickname "Hurricane Emma" for her ability to stir up controversy seemingly out of nowhere. During the day you can catch Emma bustling around the city, running errands and keeping the *Sassy Schooner* looking its best, while hubby Harold works his tail off at a plastic factory in Brampton, Ontario.

Margaret McDonald

Perhaps the most controversial houseboatwife, Margaret "Maggie" McDonald is known for being business savvy and a social butterfly. She's also known for her recent acquittal from charges related to her husband Peter's untimely death. Maggie is the sole provider for her three troublesome teens, yet balances life and work by running a small but profitable hair salon out of her houseboat *Cuttin' Cathy*, named after her mother.

Martha Russell

Townie Martha Russell is new to the neighbourhood, her husband Dale's promotion having recently brought the pair and their newborn twins to Snout Harbour. She's excited about getting to know her fellow houseboatwives, but she's a bit of an outsider in the close-knit community and is still having trouble fitting in. Even though Dale is gone six months of the year, Martha, along with her team of nannies and housekeepers, has no trouble keeping the children and *St. John's Jewel* tidy and shiny.

Margaret Morgan

The oldest boathouse on the tour, *Murphy's Sunset*, belongs to Margaret "Margie" Morgan, an empty-nester mother of six and grandmother of eleven. This self-described matriarch of Snout Harbour can be found down at the bingo hall most days, from open till lunch. The rest of the time she's throwing countless community events while simultaneously barking orders at her husband Donny, a retired lighthouse bulb replacer and founder of the Maritime Bulb Replacers Union.

1920 First public exhibition of artworks by Group of Seven; visitors must exit through gift shop

Have Your Expectations Exceeded

CANADIAN THINGS WE THOUGHT WOULD BE BAD BUT TURNED OUT OKAY

Tim Hortons Pulled Pork Sandwiches

Justin Trudeau Being Ready

Bombardier C-Series Regional Jet

Schitt's Creek

Manitoba

Primetime TVO

The Quebec Nordiques Moving to Colorado

Moving to Hamilton

MuchMoreMusic

Drake's Career

Vancouver Olympics

The Movie *Goon*

1921 Frederick Banting accidentally discovers insulin while trying to make maple syrup in his bathtub

Learn the Differences Between
Stephen Harper and Justin Trudeau

Category	Stephen Harper	Justin Trudeau
Horoscope sign	Taurus	Capricorn
Favourite Canadian band	Nickelback	Not Nickelback
Favourite sport	Writing books about hockey	Boxing
Positions on weed	Narc	Blaze it
Pop culture character he's most like	The Tin Man	Prince Eric
Bromances	Couldn't find any	Obama
Questionable fashion choices	Leather vests, his "everyman" plaid shirts, that haircut	Any time he tries to grow facial hair
First impression	He wants to make furniture using my bones	Want to jump his bones
Favourite book	*The Handmaid's Tale*	Has a lit degree, can't choose just one
What he'll be remembered for	Being Canada's first robot prime minister	First Canadian prime minister to do yoga

1922 Maple syrup prohibition ends

Hop on the Just for Laughs Death Tour

Since 2000, *Just for Laughs: Gags* has graced most Air Canada in-flight television screens and produced more than 2,500 episodes of goofy pranks, 1,200 hours of awkward silences, and a shrieking laugh track that never ceases. Each episode must pass the high standards set by the JFL Joke Lab facility, located in rural Quebec.

During their 15 seasons of filming on location in Montreal there has been a surprising number of on-set deaths, many of which are memorialized by plaques. On your next visit to the "City of Bridges," be whisked away on the JFL Gags: Musée de la mort bus tour. During the month of October, 31% of the proceeds are donated to Justice for Laughs, a foundation dedicated to compensating the families of prank- and mime-related victims.

La Fontaine Park: Le Canard Pané/ The Breaded Duck

To pull off this prank, a passerby is asked to hold the prankster's baguette while they take a selfie with the ducks in the pond. Once the prankee turns their back, the duck disappears. It's attached to a scuba diver, who surfaces, grabs the baguette out of the victim's grasp, and uses it to hit the back of their legs before fleeing the scene, loudly quacking.

Complications stemming from severe gluten intolerance resulted in prankee Gennifer Rioux's untimely death. Teenagers who make out in the park and the friendly Montreal homeless population have reported seeing the ghost of Rioux roaming the grounds and tossing quinoa into the pond.

McGill University: Le Disappearing Backpack/ The Disappearing Backpack

Convicted criminal twins Pierre and Phillippe Saints-Anges landed a role on an episode of *JFL: Gags* during its fifth season. Dressed as students, Phillippe rummaged through knapsacks, purses, and male satchels while Pierré slowly mimed about a fake petition.

Producers soon realized that their prank was poorly structured and borderline illegal after students complained about a criminal mime on campus. When the police showed up, Phillippe was Tasered following a complicated explanation that the two attempted to mime out. He died soon thereafter on location.

Place Vertu: Perdu Mall Enfants Mixup/ Lost Mall Children Mixup

In one of the most controversial episodes of *JFL: Gags'* second season, the team took over a toy shop at a mall. Wandering children were taken to the back room where they were instructed to play with an assortment of first-generation Furbys. Once their parents came looking for them, the prankster handed the parents a doll that looked exactly like their child.

JFL: Gags production assistant Hazel Rideau, who coordinated the prank, slipped on the recently polished food court floor during load-out after the mall's regular operating hours. Her lifeless body was discovered by the manager of the neighbouring Dead Sea Minerals kiosk several hours later.

Did You Know?

1 in 20 Quebec residents are currently stuck in a *Just For Laughs: Gags* freeze frame.

1924 Newfoundlander falls out of tree; the Newfie joke is invented

Add some excitement to your next social gathering by booking a MuchMusic Video Escape Room! Let our entirely ponytailed crew transform your school gymnasium into an electric circus for a truly unforgettable evening of pubescent fun. Are your middle school years behind you? No problem. We'll turn your medium-sized break room into a prison for a fun-filled afternoon of mandatory company-wide team-building activities! Amid flashing lights, pounding bass, and the simulated scent of a couple hundred gyrating 20th century tweens, will you be able to solve the puzzle and make your escape before time runs out? It's the hottest Escape Room hybrid this side of the Rideau Canal, and remember: no one wins unless you work together.

It's simple, just:

1. Determine the size of your party

We can bring the party to a minimum of a metric dozen people and a maximum of 600.

2. Call and make arrangements six weeks in advance

Remember to schedule ahead of time: summer sessions fill up fast!

3. Prepare to dance for your life

The Dance Party Escape Room lets you choose from a predetermined list of frightening scenarios sure to delight and excite your team.

SPEAKERS' HORROR

In a tiny booth redolent with the unmistakable scent of urine from Toronto's Queen and John intersection, your team will have to perform a perfect a capella rendition of the Barenaked Ladies' ubiquitous turd of a hit "One Week." Make sure you stay on key; for every bum note, you and your team will remain locked in the booth for one additional week.

GET THE NORTHERN TOUCH

This one is notorious! You'll be able to escape from this featureless room only after you locate the clues that spell out the names of every long-forgotten pre-Drake Canadian rapper featured on its classic track. If you get stuck, we'll give you Master T's cell number and you can ask him for help. Try not to overheat in that huge winter coat!

ESCAPE FROM AJAX

In a highly detailed reproduction of a suburban Toronto bedroom at the turn of the millennium, you and your team will have to solve the provided Grade 9 math problems until the answers add up to 41. How long will it take? Not long, unless it's all a mistake. Next, adjust the treble on the Panasonic Shockwave CD player until it's fully charged. If that sounds simple, that's the plan. Finally, before you earn your freedom, one member of your team must woo and eventually marry Avril Lavigne.

Did You Know?

79% of Canadian couples met at a MuchMusic Video Dance Party.

1925 The Royal Canadian Legion is formed; grandfathers everywhere spend 65% more time out of the house

Discover the Secret Messages in Fred Penner's Songs

Fred Penner has been delighting Canadian audiences for more than four decades. With his trademark blend of kid-friendly cheer and folky charm, his songs have become beloved classics for generations. Behind the friendly face, however, sinister secrets lurk. Many of Penner's most popular songs contain clandestine messages that can only be deciphered when they're played backwards. In stark contrast to his gentle reputation, the backwards messages reveal a very different side of the artist. How many of these backwards messages can you hear on your old records?

The Cat Came Back (1979): 1:22
"Kids . . . don't let your beatnik parents lead you wrong . . . the dollar, the dollar . . . we believe in the invisible hand of the powerful dollar."
Car, Car Song (1983): 2:31
"Economic growth . . . can be most effectively created by investing in capital . . . [unintelligible] . . . and through less government regulation . . . trickle down, trickle down!"
Christmas Magic (1989): 1:07
"The greatest gift of all . . . is an economic system in which transactions between private parties are free from government interference such as regulations, privileges, tariffs, and subsidies . . ."
Fred Penner's Place Theme (1990): 0:22
"Communism has been defeated by the mighty fist of capitalism, rejoice! The globe now belongs to us!"
Ebeneezer Sneezer (1992): 0:45
"Brian Mulroney! Our fearless leader! The golden age has begun . . . vote Tory, don't be sorry."
Sandwiches (1998): 2:30
"Raffi is a total jerk . . . what's the deal with that weirdo? . . . nice beard, I liked it better when it was on my face . . ."

Celebrate iCal-uit's Subtle Name Change

Warm up in the crowd at iCal-uit's only festival celebrating the city's 2014 name change. In an effort to put the lonely tundra town on the map, the capital of Nunavut changed its spelling from Iqaluit to iCal-uit after Mayor John Graham received his first iPhone, mere weeks before his resignation.

Graham, inspired by the iPhone's functionality, proposed changing the visual spelling of the city in homage to his favourite app, iCal—the default calendar included with every iOS device.

The name change is now celebrated annually. iCal Fest, sponsored by Air Inuit, is held in downtown iCal-uit and features artisan sandstone sculptors along with kiosks selling local arts and crafts and ancient preserves. Entertainment is provided by iCal-uit's own Throat Valley Singing Chorus, belting out covers of your favourite Avril jams and Edwin ballads.

Many locals opposed the name change, and these dissenters often appear at the iCal Fest to voice their objections. They're politely corralled into a designated protester area where iPhone reception is poor.

As always, iPhone charging and snowmobile parking is free, and seeing-eye sled dogs are admitted at no extra cost.

Event Services and Exhibits

Sled Dog Relief Area (Sponsored by Air Inuit)

Snowmobile Parking

D.P.A. (Designated Protester Area)

Muskox Burgers

iCal-uit Enrichment Kiosks

Throat Rap Battle

Pond Hockey Tournament

Artisanal Ice Bust Sculpting

1927 First cross-country radio broadcast: a newborn Rex Murphy mumbling

"Get Lost" at the Magnetic Triangle

The Magnetic Triangle in Monk'town (known to some as "Moncton"), New Brunswick, is for thrill seekers only—there's no telling when people, animals, and things may inexplicably disappear. And in the almost 600 recorded instances of humans vanishing in its vicinity, no one has ever escaped to tell the tale.

Controversy looms over this phenomenon, with many townspeople claiming that the government is ignoring it. Recent discoveries related to the mystery of the Magnetic Triangle have included cave etchings drawn by some of New Brunswick's earliest settlers, the tribe of Ne'erbrun. The fact remains that no one is really sure what creates the anomaly. But experts warn citizens to avoid this irregular isosceles at all costs during a storm—as depicted in this haunting New Brunswick artifact recovered in 1988 by Mrs. Brown's Grade 3 history class:

Men and horses disappear
Women and children shriek with fear
When fog rolls in with stormy clouds
Rain hellfire on Monk'town
Upon the hilltop is a knoll
Where we're told never to go
The beast of Monk'town
Opens its gills
And claims another still
And claims one more

If you're interested in finding the Magnetic Triangle (or are trying to avoid it), please refer to this map.

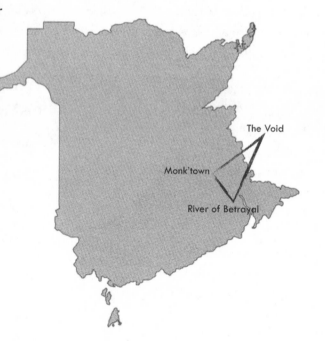

The Void

Monk'town

River of Betrayal

Learn Your Gords

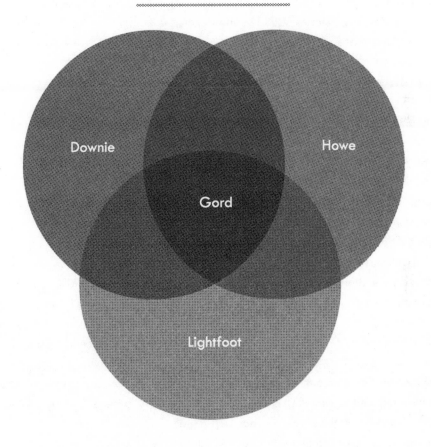

Visit the Notable Canadian–American Wax Museum

There's nothing Canadians love more than being internationally recognized. A dual Canadian–American citizenship is highly coveted, and comes with many perks:

- Free admission to Canada's Wonderland during non-peak months
- Canadian Tire Money [CTM] debit card
- Free coffee at IKEA
- Semi-private tour of the prime minister's washroom
- Tax-free cheese

If you find yourself crossing the Rainbow Bridge into Niagara Falls, Ontario, why not stop at the Notable Canadian–American Wax Museum on the better side, and find out what talented exports Canada has to offer?

Mike Myers
Dual citizen percentage: 65% CDN, 35% US
Although the actor still bravely touts a Leafs jersey, Canada has not been thrilled since his performance in and overall insistence on making of *The Love Guru*.

Conrad Black
Dual citizen percentage: 45% CDN, 55% US
Born in Canada, Conrad Black fathered the conservative rag the *National Post*. He served three-and-a-half years of a six-year prison sentence in the United States before being deported to Canada and slapped with a 30-year re-entry ban. Canadians have not forgiven Black for renouncing his Canadian citizenship in favour of a fancy British title back in 2001.

Kim Cattrall
Dual citizen percentage: 90% CDN, 10% US
Born in England, Cattrall immigrated to Canada with her family when she was three. Most Canadians agree that Cattrall's portrayal of Samantha Jones in *Sex and the City* is by far her career highlight, after her brief fling with Pierre Trudeau, of course.

Jim Carrey
Dual citizen percentage: 20% CDN, 80% US
Carrey's stint as an anti-vaxxer has tainted the image of the comedic actor for many Canadians.

1929 Stock market crash prompts most Canadians to switch their savings to hockey cards

Sandra Oh

Dual citizen percentage: 72% CDN, 28% US
Statistics show that 45% of Canadians can correctly identify Sandra Oh as one of the characters from the movie *Sideways*, and that although Canadians overall know nothing about Sandra Oh, they are 100% confident in educating friends and family about Oh's birthplace.

Randy Quaid

Dual citizen percentage: 7% CDN, 93% US
Quaid was granted refuge in Canada after claiming he was on the run from the "Hollywood Star Whackers." He was unsuccessfully exiled to the United States over vandalism and an unpaid $10,000 hotel bill in California, and eventually fled for Vermont in 2015.

Ted Cruz

Dual citizen percentage: 1% CDN, 99% US
American politician Teddy C renounced his Canadian citizenship in 2014 after scrutiny of his dual status, though it was revealed that he hadn't realized he held Canadian citizenship in the first place.

Matthew Perry

Dual citizen percentage: 20% CDN, 80% US
Most Canadians assume Perry is Canadian since he's only been photographed while wearing a Senators jersey. In actual fact, Matthew Perry was born in the States and raised in our nation's capital, later working on a television show about Toronto's cool older brother, New York City.

Did You Know?

The average Canadian media personality is three times homelier than their American counterpart.

1930 First female senator, Cairine Wilson, massively exceeds expectations for such an innocuous position

Pick Up a Copy of Canada's Steamiest Hockey Erotica Series

In a Kingston, Ontario, retirement home lives a local woman who goes by the nom de plume "Mary Cherry." She's 89, and Canada's oldest living erotica writer. After the death of her husband, Mary made several attempts at time-killing hobbies, but felt that she was young at heart and that most hobbies for her demographic were boring.

Mary's luck changed when her son dumped off a box of old VHS tapes, including several *Rock'em Sock'em Hockey* cassettes. She developed what might be considered a "crush" on its host and began writing steamy, hockey-related erotic novels centred on Canada's phlegmiest talking bowling pin, Don Cherry. We sent a researcher to talk to Mary about her important contribution to Canadian literature:

What is it about Don Cherry that you love?

His hearty grunt, incessant cough, and the hoarseness in his voice after a good scream.

Is there a reason why Mr. Cherry seems to always come down with the flu in your novels?

As I always say, plugging Cold FX is never inappropriate. It's a fantastic product that I can proudly say I use, sometimes when I'm sick, and sometimes when there's ice on the roads and the cabinets are bare.

What should fans expect from your next book?

A real team effort, pinko or not, it's for the everyday Canadian and I'm going to give it 110%.

Here are some excerpts from some of Cherry's sauciest works:

1931 Unemployment hits 30%; Canada moves back into Mom and Dad's basement

Sensual Stanley: One Cup, One Heart

"It was the playoffs. Mr. Cherry was furious and had the flu as usual. I fixed him his favourite: two shots of Jameson and four shots of Cold FX, garnished with a lemon wedge. The honey came later and I needed to throw out another set of sticky sheets, dear me."

Snowed-In Saturday

"It was a Saturday evening during a snowstorm, after Don braved 72 hours of Norovirus followed by his third brush with shingles. He couldn't wait to get into my corners. And since he couldn't get the game to work on the iPad, all eyes were on me."

Back Bacon Brunch Booty Call

"Don spent the night and I wanted to fix him a quick breakfast in bed before my girlfriend Susan came over for our bridge game—she can be so judgmental. I heard his distinct toady growl over the sizzling bacon and it was then that I knew the bronchitis was back and was here to stay."

Desperate Measures

"There was a trail of plaid leading to the bedroom and I could smell the familiar mixture of sweat and Gold Bold. It was Don, grunting over his hot toddy. He had the flu and was shamelessly sweating it out in the living room."

The Hungry, Hungry Hunk

"I awoke, suddenly, in the empty living room. SunTV was on mute and two Hungry Man TV dinners sat steaming on the coffee table. 'You can't have creamed corn without ketchup,' he said, startling me. He took a swig of Cold FX out of the bottle on his bedside table. It was the flu again."

$1932 The most you should pay for a chesterfield →

Canada, a nation founded in 1867, did not consider women to be "persons" until 1929. Canadian women today should feel great about being officially recognized as living humans for a slight majority of the country's history, but in the embarrassingly recent past that non-recognition had led to a lot of confusion, with many women wondering what they were if not persons.

Meanwhile, the long march to women's suffrage that had begun in the 1800s continued, stepping over upset men as it went. It wasn't until 1960 that Canadian women were granted the right to vote in federal and provincial elections (an affirmation analogous to the long Canadian "Oh yeah, the Indigenous people were here first so maybe we should finally give them some rights" tradition).

Although women made up 50% of the population of Canada, men controlled 100% of the rights. In the years before gaining suffrage, women had been performing a number of jobs, including but not limited to cooking, gardening, factory work, farming, and generally many of the same tasks men did but with little to no pay or recognition. Another fine 19th century tradition that, like moustaches and artisanal candle making, has persisted in Canada and around the world.

Women won the right to stand for the House of Commons in 1919, although appointment to the Senate remained out of

Why Women Were Not Allowed to Vote

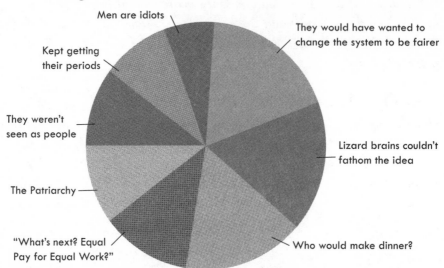

Men are idiots

Kept getting their periods

They weren't seen as people

The Patriarchy

"What's next? Equal Pay for Equal Work?"

They would have wanted to change the system to be fairer

Lizard brains couldn't fathom the idea

Who would make dinner?

reach until the aforementioned Persons Case of 1929, which is like saying to someone, "Hey, you can be on the Toronto Maple Leafs if you try out, but you're not allowed to ever try out," and then patting yourself on the back.

Two years before that, in 1927, five women from Alberta had banded together to petition the Supreme Court on the issue. They came to be known as "The Famous Five" after "The Spice Girls" didn't test well. On Parliament Hill there now stands a group of statues representing Emily Murphy, Irene Marryat Parlby, Nellie McClung, Louise Crummy McKinney, and Henrietta Muir Edwards in their efforts to get the Supreme Court to finally answer the question of whether women should be persons. The women are depicted with stoic, determined expressions, and some observers feel they should smile more.

The Famous Five statues have become a popular place for kids to hang out and Snapchat, since there aren't many other places to go in Ottawa after business hours. Often spotted at the monument are a gang of feral cats, the lonely mascot of the long-defunct Ottawa Lynx baseball team, and Justin Trudeau just sitting around on his lunch break. After you visit, make sure to take the Buzzfeed quiz "What Famous Canadian Suffragette Are You?" It is estimated that, after tourists visit the monument, only 11% still feel compelled to post #NotAllMen on Twitter or explain to a woman why catcalling is actually a compliment.

What Were Women If They Were Not Persons?

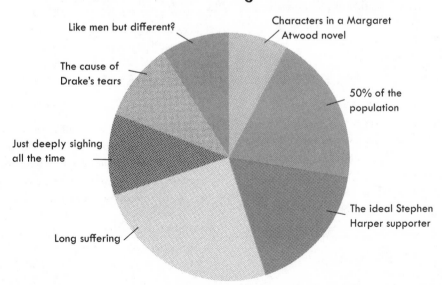

Like men but different?

The cause of Drake's tears

Just deeply sighing all the time

Long suffering

Characters in a Margaret Atwood novel

50% of the population

The ideal Stephen Harper supporter

Eat a Donair: A How-To Guide

Each year, 7.3 million donairs are consumed in Nova Scotia. Every three seconds someone from Nova Scotia eats another one. It is the great epidemic affecting the waistlines of people from Yarmouth to Pleasant Bay (which is, actually, only about 36% pleasant). But they're delicious and the people cannot be denied.

Since these treats haven't yet translated to much of the rest of Canada, we've compiled a how-to guide on the do-nairs and do-nots of eating a donair.

Step One: Determine your method of transportation to the donair restaurant. Do not be ambitious and think you can bike there and back. Remember that you'll be much heavier once your belly is filled with condensed milk, garlic powder, and vinegar. Remember also to consider the return trip. 17% of traffic accidents in Nova Scotia occur because of drivers who have eaten too many donairs and fallen asleep at the wheel.

Step Two: Wear pants with an elastic waist. Jeans are not compatible with donairs.

Step Three: Once you arrive at your location, scope out the restaurant. You will not want to sit in a spot that draws too much attention to your gluttony. Pick a table near the back, preferably in the shadows where you can indulge guilt-free.

Step Four: Time to order. The donair typically consists of heavily sliced ground beef placed in a pita with tomatoes and raw onions (accounting for why so many Nova Scotians have been burdened with the nickname "Onion Breath"). The donair is then soaked in donair sauce (evaporated milk, vinegar, garlic powder, sugar). Finally, the unholy amalgam is wrapped in tinfoil and handed across the counter.

Step Five: Place a handful of napkins in the collar of your shirt. This will serve as a net for any sauces dribbling down your chin. In 1992, in an effort to reduce the amount of waste these napkin nets created, the government of Nova Scotia produced reusable napkin collars that could be washed and worn for multiple trips back to the donair shop. 87% of residents rejected these as "gross" and the project was abandoned.

Step Six: Find a position that works for you. Sometimes it's easiest to lean forward to make sure you get it all into your mouth. Put the donair in your mouth (don't neglect the tip!) and bite down. Chew carefully; you'll want to savour all the meat and juices. Really move your tongue around to experience the different flavours. And make some noise while eating to show the chef your appreciation!

Step Seven: Once you're finished you'll probably find a mess of sauces all over your chin. You'll want to use your napkin collar to wipe yourself off. Thank the spirit of your donair for providing you with so much pleasure. It has served you well.

Donair Fact: 99% of donairs are eaten after 2 a.m. by drunk people.

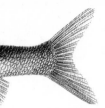

Bring Back Souvenirs from the Maritimes

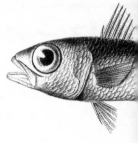

The Maritimes! Fish! Beer! Other things they're known for! You'll want to capture the best of Canada's most picturesquely impoverished provinces in the souvenirs you bring back for you, your friends, and your family. Our research shows that 72% of friends can tell that the St. John's coffee mug they got was an afterthought purchased at the airport. We've compiled a list of the best souvenirs to bring home after a trip to Canada's delightful East Coast.

Way more fish than you're legally allowed to bring on a plane

Five air fresheners to try to cover the smell of the fish

Miniature lighthouse keychains for the coworkers you don't know very well

A bottle of tap water from Cole Harbour just in case it *is* in the water there

Donair sauce

Three potatoes

The bulb from the Peggy's Cove lighthouse

A sweatshirt that says Cape Breton on the front that you hope hides the fact that you forgot to get a personalized souvenir but at least this is better than nothing, right?

An Anne of Green Gables impersonator you've kidnapped

Framed picture of you standing next to the Dildo town sign in Newfoundland

Pirate bones from Hangman's Beach

The shirt you wore to the Alexander Keith's brewery tour that you threw up on because you insisted on doing the tour after you ate three lobster rolls and you didn't think that would be a problem

1934 The Statute of Westminster deeply offends King George

Get Invited to a Cottage

There are few activities more Canadian than loading up on carbs while sitting on a dock. The most recent census of Canadian long weekend activities indicates that the average citizen consumes one entire bag of ketchup chips for every six bottles of Molson Canadian. As soon as the thermometer reaches double digits and the last snowbank transforms into a filthy puddle of trash, the race to get to the cottage is on.

The easiest, most organic way of getting invited to a cottage is to become friends with someone who has a cottage. Sure, while some might consider it manipulative to befriend a person just for access to their fancy summertime vacation house, if you do it far enough in advance they'll never know and you'll be laughing all the way to Muskoka.

The prime summer cottaging months are between June and early September. Thus, you'll want to start laying the seeds of new friendship by February at the latest. You need time to really become invested in this person's cottage, oops, *life* before you even begin to broach the subject of a weekend getaway. This will take time if you want to build a long-lasting, meaningful, open invitation to their cottage.

In the end, all those months of pretending to care about this person will pay off when you're escaping the city for a weekend filled with sun, water, and lots and lots of alcohol.

Tips for Getting That Cottage Invite

- Don't start a conversation with "Do you have a cottage?" If their answer is yes, they'll be suspicious as to why you want to know, and if the answer is no, they'll be offended when you immediately walk away in search of your next potential new friend.

- Creep them on Instagram to make sure that they do, in fact, have a cottage! Make sure they have their own lakefront property. Don't waste your time befriending someone when they've actually only just visited their friend's cottage.

1935 Canadian Wheat Board is created, forming a powerful shadow government that still controls Canada

- Ask to see pictures of your new friend's cottage. Wistfully murmur phrases like "I'd love to stand on that dock as the sun sets" and "I bet you have some great campfires there. Did you know I make a mean s'more?"

- Casually mention to your new friend that you have no plans for the weekend and are really in need of some relaxation and sure would love to get out of the city for a few days. This works even better if you overhear them mentioning to someone else that they're planning to head up to their cottage for the weekend. Insert yourself into that conversation and get that invite!

Disclaimer: If you're friends with anyone who works at Stats Canada, we are definitely not using you for your cottage. We like you for you.

Cottage Packing List

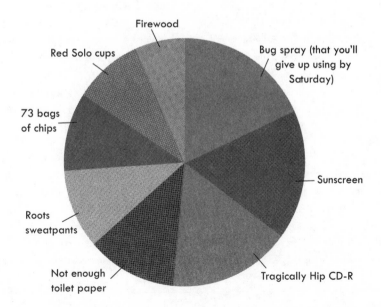

1936 The CBC is created, giving rise to Canada's liberal elite

Discover Canadian Wildlife

Canada is home to a great variety of wildlife species, and many have become synonymous with the Canadian identity. Beyond our borders, plenty of people would identify a beaver, or a blue jay, or even a polar bear as being distinctly Canadian. However, Canada is such a vast country that the list of fauna cannot stop there.

Here we list a few of the lesser-known species of Canadian wildlife in order to shed some light on other great creatures, big and small, that make this country beautiful.

The Ryan Gosling (*Sraecalfactus sapidum masculum*): Covered from bill to foot in fluffy yellow down, the Ryan Gosling induces Canadians across the nation to exclaim "Awwww" and then get all hot and bothered.

The IKEA Monkey (*Decorus tunicam simia*): The IKEA Monkey is often spotted wandering the halls of suburban IKEAs wearing a miniature shearling jacket and a bewildered expression. It is believed that only one remains in all of Canada. Estimates vary, however, as what happens in IKEA stays in IKEA. The IKEA Monkey makes its home among Bjursta tables and Smörboll duvet covers and couples arguing.

The Canada Goose (*Simplex facile feminam*): This basic creature can be spotted at Starbucks across the nation sporting its trademark black coat and coyote fur. The Canada Goose's mating call consists of a shrill "I can't even," usually uttered at something mundane, and "Oh. My. God." The Canada Goose is considered far from extinct and is practically running amok in the highly populated areas of Toronto, Vancouver, and Montreal.

Polkaroo (*Formidulosis procerus et ridiculum*): A spotted, lumbering splice between a kangaroo and the beloved green humanoid Gumby.

Bonhomme (*Qntal creaturae*): "Creepy," "spooky," and "scary" are all adjectives used to describe the oddly shaped nightmare monster from Quebec. His slight smile hides a sinister, murderous being that has terrified children since he began his tenure as the Quebec City Winter Festival's mascot. Considered one of Canada's most frightening beasts, Bonhomme is not one to be crossed and should be avoided at all costs. [*Editor's Note:* Do not whisper "Bonhomme" three times into a reflective ice sculpture lest he appear and slaughter you.]

Ananas (*Sermo fructus*): This yellow, warty, pineapple-shaped animal is native to rural Quebec. The Ananas—whose laissez-faire temperament makes for an ideal elementary-level French-language teaching aide—is featured in the *Téléfrançais* TV show, which began airing a few years after the 1980 Quebec referendum as Québécois propaganda meant to brainwash the young English-speaking minds of Canada.

The Kroeger (*Turpe capillos yello*): One of Canada's ugliest creatures, the Kroeger is found largely in the vicinity of monster truck rallies and trailer parks across the prairies. Known primarily for its loud, squawking, repetitive mating call, the Kroeger inexplicably manages to find mates. And yet no one admits to enjoying the Kroeger.

1937 Canada reaches peak hat

Identify Toronto's Pests

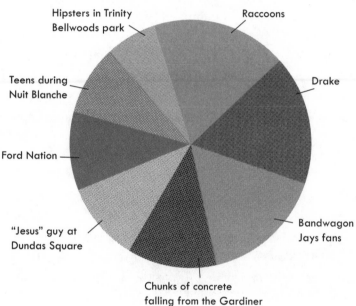

Hipsters in Trinity Bellwoods park

Raccoons

Teens during Nuit Blanche

Drake

Ford Nation

"Jesus" guy at Dundas Square

Bandwagon Jays fans

Chunks of concrete falling from the Gardiner

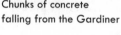

1938 Parliament passes Lowest Price Is the Law

Visit the Abandoned Shania Twain Centre

The Shania Twain Centre was a museum dedicated to all things Shania in her hometown of Timmins, Ontario. When it opened in June 2001, museum officials optimistically saw a need for an entire centre devoted to the pop singer. However, times grew tough for the Northern Ontario museum. Shania Twain herself did not personally visit it until 2004, although the residents of Timmins found this understandable—why would anyone leave their chalet in Switzerland for Timmins?

Museum Highlights

The 2006 fan convention that her fiddler attended

The stage from her UP! tour

An actual lock of her hair. Well, it could have been her hair. There's really no way to say this isn't a lock of her hair. It's brown, and she has brown hair. What more proof do you need, Brenda?

The Toronto Maple Leafs jersey she wore during a Toronto concert and then threw on the ice

A Grammy with a piece of Scotch tape covering Alanis Morissette's name

The museum was never quite able to attract visitors. Common complaints:

- "Why would I ever travel all the way to Timmins to look at a sweaty sequined crop top?"
- "The museum smells like feet and a raccoon sleeps in the tour bus."
- "I'm really more of an Anne Murray fan."

It was estimated that the museum lost about 98% of the money invested.

Shania had a complicated history with the museum, and upon starting her Vegas residency she took back the stage and tour bus she had donated. However, the lock of hair remained at the museum. Shania was quoted as saying, "That's not my hair."

The museum shuttered its doors in 2013 after a decade of decreasing visitors every year. Dozens of fans were devastated, and reportedly chained themselves to a life-sized Shania Twain cardboard cutout in front of the centre in hopes of reversing the decision. The protest ended swiftly when it started to rain and the Shania cutout became a soggy pile of mush. Remaining items of Shania memorabilia were dispersed to the city's airport and library. The lock of hair has since gone missing.

In 2015 town officials sold the building and a Coffee Time was opened in what had once been the museum. More people attended the opening of the franchise than had ever visited the Shania Twain Centre. Local controversy ensued when upset Shania fans broke in and began squatting in the Coffee Time in an operation that became known as Occupy Shania. This protest lasted for two days until the occupants stumbled upon the corpse of a raccoon that had been living in the tour bus.

Shania Twain's Ideal Man

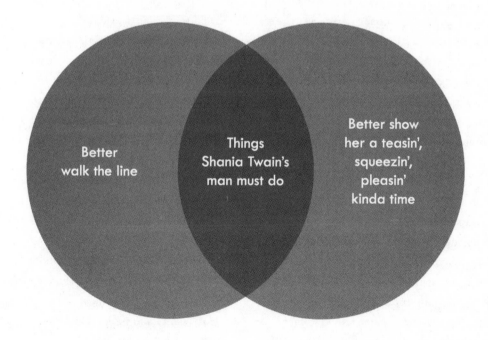

Better walk the line

Things Shania Twain's man must do

Better show her a teasin', squeezin', pleasin' kinda time

1940 What is the year in which Alex Trebek was born?

Read a Forgotten Heather's Pick

Avid Canadian readers who've spent enough time wandering around an Indigo or Chapters store will recognize on book covers the gold sticker proclaiming "Heather's Pick" (or, "You will like this guaranteed or you can return it at any point, even if it's been 10 years and you've spilled a little wine on it and you're actually not even sure how you ended up with this copy of *The Lovely Bones*. You kind of thought the movie was better but you didn't tell anyone because you didn't want to look dumb. Mark Wahlberg was a little miscast, though, if we're going to be honest. Anyway, here's your money back. Full refund").

Heather Reisman is the Canadian founder of the Indigo chain, which many Canadians know as the bookstore that is 35% scented candles, 20% cute throw pillows, 25% decorative plates, and 20% books. As CEO, Heather is like a Canadian Oprah, bestowing a golden sticker upon her favourite titles to show she has approved. These picks usually receive a spike in sales, which leads to a lot of authors trying to curry her favour through compliments and baked goods.

Over time Heather has amassed a lengthy list of sure-to-be bestsellers, but some have been forgotten owing to time and the popularity of Netflix and the fact that Twitter has ruined the literary attention spans of millennials. Here's a list of some of her less popular picks over the years:

- *Another Short Story About Land* by Alice Munro
- *Where Have All the Veejays Gone?* by Rick the Temp
- *If I Did It: Confessions of the Killer* by Stephen Harper
- A book about money from one of those dudes on *Dragons' Den*
- *C U L8r, Hater* by Avril Lavigne
- A coffee table book featuring pictures of children skating on ice rinks
- Another coffee table book featuring pictures of children skating on ice rinks
- *I Know You Pretended to Read The English Patient* by Michael Ondaatje
- *Stats Canada: Satire on a National Scale*
- *Please Don't Call This Sci-Fi* by Margaret Atwood
- Something that was nominated for the Giller
- *My Voice Is Actually High-Pitched in Real Life* by Peter Mansbridge
- *I Didn't Sleep with a Bear* by Marian Engel
- *The Wilderness Is Tough* by Farley Mowat
- A novelization of the movie *Goon*
- *Not Even Going to Pretend I Helped Write This One* by Justin Bieber

1941 Tillie Hosken of Toronto is the first woman to score 450 in five-pin bowling

Search the Web, Canadian Style

Although the Canadian Radio-television and Telecommunications Commission (CRTC) requires all Canadians to depend on SaskJeeves for their web searches, many Canadians use a proxy to illegally access Google. We hacked the mainframe to gather this summary of the most frequently searched terms by Canadians.

Top Canadian Web Searches

How to get American Netflix?
Cute pics of Justin Trudeau shirtless
How to skate faster
Is Sarah McLachlan single?
Why is it so cold?
Is it supposed to snow in June?
Is it supposed to snow in July?
Is it supposed to snow in August?
BC weed
How long are you legally allowed to stay in a Tim Hortons?
What do the Kids in the Hall look like now?
How does the luge work?
Lyrics to Snow's "Informer"
Paulina Gretzky
Videos of hockey fights
"Let's Go to the Mall" lyrics
Is Santa Canadian?

1942 Cabbage becomes a very popular soup

Visit Alberta's Gopher Hole Museum

Located in beautiful Torrington, Alberta, the Gopher Hole Museum is the most fun you'll ever have looking at dead, stuffed, and costumed rodents. Since its opening in 1996, the museum has been a haven for tourists seeking out "the weirdest possible thing to Instagram" while on a trip to Canada's fourth most-populated province.

Over 71 gophers are on display. They're dressed in dazzling costumes—from Mountie to priest to fisherman—and placed upon creative backgrounds. Although it takes only about 10 minutes to peruse the entire museum, many visitors have reported seeing these creatures in their "worst nightmares," which makes the $2 entrance fee a real bargain!

When the museum first opened, PETA called for a boycott. This increased visitation by 83%. The museum sent PETA a postcard signed "Get stuffed," which is the gentlest rebuff PETA has ever received.

Abandoned Gopher Models

JUSTIN BIEBER MEETING STEPHEN HARPER WHILE WEARING OVERALLS: This moment in Canadian history was considered too embarrassing to replicate, even with dead gophers in costumes.

THE EPISODE OF *DEGRASSI* WHERE JIMMY GETS SHOT: The artist had to relinquish this model when he couldn't get the gopher's legs into a sitting position for the mini-wheelchair.

GRETZKY CRYING AFTER BEING TRADED TO L.A.: Having crafted this sculpture to pay tribute to Edmonton's favourite Oiler, the artist completely destroyed it with his own tears.

ANNE OF GREEN GABLES AND HER FRIEND DIANA: During a brief period in the early 00s, the museum experimented with a "Gopher Hole Museum: After Dark" theme, at which point the gopher dioramas took a more salacious turn and featured the beloved literary character doing indecent things. The diorama was quickly shelved owing to lawsuit threats, concerned parents, and the return of common sense.

Tell Someone Ellen Page Is from Nova Scotia

Did you know Ellen Page is from Nova Scotia?

yes

no

You do now!

See Someone Who Was on *Degrassi*

The wildly successful *Degrassi* franchise has been broadcast on Canadian television since before Wheelchair Jimmy was Wheelchair Jimmy. Every Canadian has their favourite series (*Degrassi: The Next Generation*) and their favourite *Degrassi* alum (Ellie Nash, obviously). Every Canadian also has an anecdote about the time they saw someone in real life who was on *Degrassi*.

You haven't experienced the real Toronto until you've been walking down Bloor Street and had to stop to excitedly text your friend, "I think I just saw Manny Santos!!!"

Stats Fact: 96% of Torontonians have been an extra on *Degrassi*.

Did You Know?

The most watched television episode in Canadian history was the *Degrassi* reunion on *Jonovision*.

Try Every Type of Poutine

Everyone loves poutine. It's a Canadian delicacy because you can eat it whenever, wherever, however. It's the down-to-earth food that unites the nation. Most people go for the gravy, cheese curds, and fries staple, but we here at Stats Canada say, "Hey, why not mix it up?" We've conducted a major poutine census to collect some lesser-known favourites from throughout this great country. Try them all and gain seven pounds and a cholesterol problem!

The Céline: Light on the fries, heavy on the cheese. Your heart will go on and on until it gives out from all the curds.

The Cheese Bacon Curds (CBC): The government funds a percentage of this dish and you have to watch three episodes of *Corner Gas* while consuming it.

The 6: Big in Ontario. The rest of Canada doesn't really see the appeal. Drake acts like he invented it.

The Double-Double: This is when you eat one poutine and then order another because it's one in the morning and you're drunk and this seems like a good idea.

Heather's Pick: We guarantee these great Heather's Pick poutines or you'll receive a full refund!

The Bieber: When ordering this one you keep it quiet from your friends. You don't tell anyone that you actually kind of like it and that it's transcended being a guilty pleasure and you actively enjoy it now, but you understand why it is bad for you.

The Separatist Special: Order this and you get to eat it in your own corner of the restaurant while everyone else glares at you because really? We're doing this again, Jacques?

The Maple Bacon Leafs: Loaded up with maple bacon, hugely expensive, ultimately disappoint-ing, and yet every time you order it you get excited, thinking, "This time it's gonna be good. This time I won't be disappointed."

Prairie Doggin': This one is pretty self-explanatory, and actually, upon further reflection, it's pretty gross to name a poutine after what happens after you eat it. Stats Canada does not recommend this one.

2112: Named after a Rush song because just when you think this poutine buffet must be over, there's even more.

1945 Canada destroys final enemy; nation doesn't know what to do with itself

Read a Forgotten Buzzfeed Canada Article

- 17 Times the Canadian Side of Niagara Falls Was Better
- 10 Prince Edward Island Lighthouses That Look Exactly Like Dicks
- 25 Tumbleweeds That You Won't Believe Look Just Like Peter Mansbridge
- 12 of the Hottest Drifters You'll See on the Trans-Canada Highway
- 69 Hot Photos of Total Bae Justin Trudeau! Like OMG!
- 13 Ways Anne of Green Gables Was #squadgoals
- 16 of the Hottest Pictures of Stephen Harper with a Drawn-On Hitler Moustache
- 8 Times Your Dad Embarrassed You by Wearing a Canadian Tuxedo
- 8 Sexy Before and After Photos of Canada's Melting Polar Ice Caps
- The 13 Times Justin Bieber DIDN'T Spit on a Homeless Person!
- 11 Historic Toronto Buildings That Will Soon Be Condos
- 17 Small-Town Gas Stations That Could Have Been Used for the *Corner Gas* Set but Ultimately Were Not Chosen
- 12 New Ways to Apologize for When Someone Bumps into You
- 8 Times the Toronto Maple Leafs Didn't Have an Embarrassing Playoff Collapse AND the 26 Times They Did!
- 31 Epic Margaret Atwood Twitter Burns
- 17 Weird Smells at the Cottage
- 16 Times Linda at Mr. Sub Forgot the Pickles on Your Sub
- 10 Our Lady Peace Songs That Are Secretly About Pooping Your Pants

1946 Canada Savings Bond introduced; a $100 bond purchased in 1946 would be worth $117 today

Have a Million Dollars (2017 Update)

A million dollars doesn't go as far as it used to. According to the most recent census of irritating Canadian adult-oriented pop-rock groups, here are the most popular ways to spend a metric megaloonie.

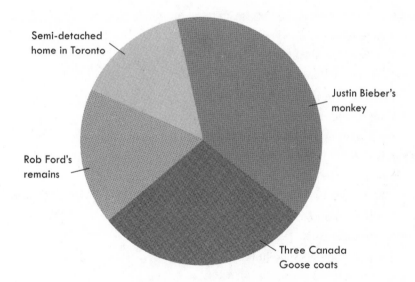

Semi-detached home in Toronto

Justin Bieber's monkey

Rob Ford's remains

Three Canada Goose coats

1947 Oil discovered in Leduc, Alberta

Things Whiter Than Newfoundland

Newfoundland and Labrador is Canada's most linguistically homogeneous province, with 97% of residents reporting their first language as English, which statistically correlates to a whole lot of pale legs and bad dancing. But rather than paint the whole island with a white brush, we wanted to gain perspective and find things that were just a little bit whiter than Canada's youngest province.

- A Stephen Harper rally
- The Fleetwood Mac reunion tour
- Canada's melting polar ice caps
- The campus of Western University
- The lyrics to any Gordon Lightfoot song
- The crowd at the ACC when the Leafs play
- Any Toronto brunch spot
- Members of Parliament
- A Facebook comment section on an article about the War on Christmas
- The set of *Road to Avonlea*
- Nickelback fans
- Steven Page's cocaine habit

1948 Baby boomers begin slow plot to wreck economy

Have It Your Way at Harvey's

In an effort to stand out in the crowded Canadian fast-food marketplace, Harvey's has been letting customers have it their way by allowing them to bring in their own toppings and condiments.

In 2008, Harvey's surveyed consumers across the 10 provinces and Home Depots in which it currently operates to find out what items Canadians prefer on their burger.

Your Way	British Columbia	Alberta	Saskatchewan	Manitoba	Ontario
#1 Topping	Smoked salmon	Cow bun	Perogy	Pickerel	Maple syrup
#2 Topping	Nanaimo bar crumbs	Diced steak	Saskatoon berry jam	Pea soup	Jerk chicken
#3 Topping	Seaweed compote	Ketchup gravy	Deer pemmican	Bannock bun	Leftover shawarma
Your Way	Quebec	Nova Scotia	New Brunswick	PEI	Newfoundland
#1 Topping	Smoked meat	Donair sauce	Unidentifiable hoof	Scalloped potatoes	Sack of boiled vegetables
#2 Topping	Montreal bagel bun	Chunked lobster	Blood of thine enemies	Pea soup	Lager reduction
#3 Topping	Baked beans	Tartar sauce	Pickled fiddlehead	Boiled potato	Whatever's available

The results were as varied and diverse as the nation itself. So, for Harvey's 50th birthday in 2009, the franchise decided to take one condiment from every province and create "Canada's favourite burger."

The beautiful mosaic of flavours stood out from the melting pot experiments of Harvey's American fast-food competitors. It also helped drive the chain's market share to heretofore unseen heights. Today, Harvey's enjoys a lofty status as the sixth most popular dining option in Canadian university cafeterias, one spot above Mr. Sub and only slightly behind "[defeated sigh] I guess I'll just have a granola bar or something."

Stats Fact: 74% of Canadians have consensually had their way with Ron the manager in a Harvey's washroom.

1949 Newfoundland joins Canada; half of population immediately moves to Leduc, Alberta

Take the Bus Instead

In large Canadian cities, many citizens prefer to stretch the meaning of personal space by utilizing public transit to commute to work, school, or ringette practice. Sometimes the best way to see a city is through the eyes of someone who lives there, and what better way than spending an hour of your time sharing air with 50 complete strangers?

Find out if local transit is right for you with our handy chart.

Vancouver TransLink
Adult fare: $2.75
Pros: Impromptu hippie drum circles
Risks: Flash flooding

Edmonton Transit System
Adult fare: $3.25
Pros: Hop on and off easily for frozen yogurt and shoes
Risks: The entire bus system exists only within the West Edmonton Mall

Calgary Transit
Adult fare: $3.15
Pros: Every bus is just 12 cows tied together
Risks: Largest public-transit BSE outbreak

Regina Transit
Adult fare: $3.00
Pros: Now air-conditioned
Risks: Losing your R-card

Saskatoon Transit
Adult fare: $3.00
Pros: Newly carpeted ceilings and walls
Risks: Low ridership cancellations, wheat blindness

Winnipeg Transit
Adult fare: $2.65
Pros: Igloo bus stops
Risks: Bus-stop polar bear encounters

Toronto Transit Commission
Adult fare: $3.25
Pros: Heightened smell tolerance, timeless door chime
Risks: Dufferin bus psychosis

OC Transpo (Ottawa)
Adult fare: $3.65
Pros: Improve your balance and coordination by standing inside the accordion part of the bus
Risks: Getting stuck in a conversation with a civil servant

1950 Major flooding in Winnipeg causes severe dampness

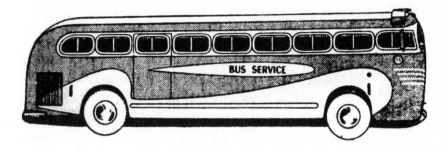

Société de transport de Montréal
Adult fare: $3.25
Pros: Smoking allowed
Risks: *Just for Laughs* gaggery

Ne'erbrun Codiac Transit
Adult fare: 2.25 doubloonies
Pros: All-boat transportation
Risks: Scurvy, boat jitters, seasickness

Charlottetown T3
Adult fare: $2.25
Pros: Short and fast routes
Risks: Amphibious bus during non-peak
hours Monday—Friday, all day Saturday &
Sunday

Halifax Transit
Adult fare: $2.50
Pros: Fiddle stowaway
Risks: Leaving your fiddle on the bus

St. John's Metrobus
Adult fare: $2.25
Pros: Returnable empties
Risks: Stale beer scent

Yellowknife Public Transit
Adult fare: $3.00
Pros: Panoramic bus windows
Risks: Polar bear bites

Whitehorse Transit
Adult fare: $2.50
Pros: Snowmobile towing
Risks: Missing the only bus

Iqaluit Public Transit
Adult fare: $480.25
Pros: It's actually an airplane
Risks: Landing a plane in Iqaluit is hazard-
ous during bear season

1951 Jeff Hyslop, star of *Today's Special*, is born

Ask for the Prime Minister's Special

Among the prime minister's many solemn obligations (shepherding legislation through the House, guiding the nation in times of crisis, providing a jump to any Canadian with a dead car battery) is making a personal appearance at the opening of every new restaurant. To show their appreciation, all Canadian restaurant chains have a "Prime Minister's Special"—you won't find it on the menu, but any Canadian can order it.

Boston Pizza

A personal pizza piled high with a delicate compromise of Quebec cheese, prairie wheat crust, and Alberta beef, handmade by a laid-off Ontario autoworker.

Tim Hortons

Triple-stacked grilled panini, layered with maple-encrusted peameal bacon and ham.

Country Style Coffee

A medium cup of lukewarm coffee poured into a large cup promoting the Turn Up a Winner contest that ended months before.

Swiss Chalet

Ten minutes alone with the Swiss Chalet treasure box.

Harvey's (Home Depot locations only)

Simply mention the Prime Minister's Special and the Harvey's shift supervisor will let you toss a sack of rustic potatoes into a Home Depot wood chipper.

Moxie's Grill & Bar

Korean shortribs swimming in a steaming hot bowl of broccoli and cashew cheddar soup. Primoxie your meal with a maple gooseberry moxitini.

Pickle Barrel

Sitting prime ministers are permitted to select their own pickle by plunging their arm elbow-deep into the pickle barrel itself.

Mandarin

Next time you're at a Mandarin buffet, help yourself to the PMS by pressing the button hidden beneath the steam tray of chicken fingers. An official buffet concierge will appear, allowing you to skip to the front of any line and select your morsels of surf and/ or turf with a gilded pair of tongs (offer not valid during CrabFest).

Earl's

The Prime Minister's Special is the only way to actually leave, as there is no exit from Earl's. Whisper the prime minister's name and they'll let you into the employee washroom. If you can fit through the window, you're free.

How Is Stephen Harper Spending His Free Time

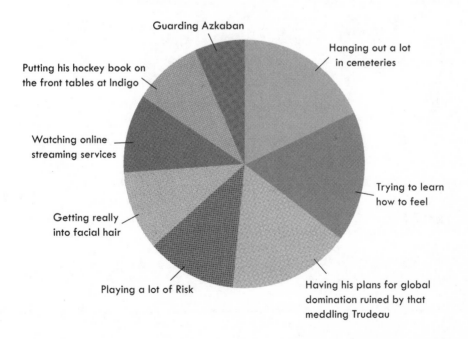

Guarding Azkaban

Hanging out a lot in cemeteries

Putting his hockey book on the front tables at Indigo

Watching online streaming services

Trying to learn how to feel

Getting really into facial hair

Playing a lot of Risk

Having his plans for global domination ruined by that meddling Trudeau

1953 Canada says "No thank you" to rock 'n' roll

Learn to Love Saskatchewan

Canada's flattest province has more to love than TV's Brent Butt. Check out the top things people love about Saskatchewan.

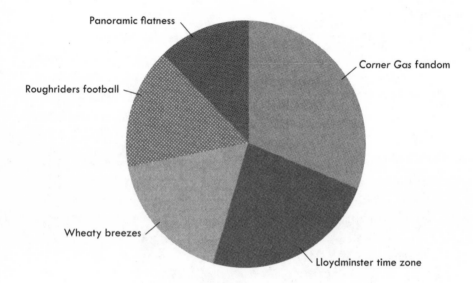

Panoramic flatness

Corner Gas fandom

Roughriders football

Wheaty breezes

Lloydminster time zone

Repurpose the Rideau Canal

Connecting the Ottawa River to the mighty St. Lawrence, the Rideau Canal was constructed in 1832 as a defensive precaution in case of war with the United States. But now that America is a close friend that only occasionally allows a dangerous demagogue to twitter-troll his way to the presidency, the Rideau Canal has little purpose. A glorified ditch in summer and too narrow for hockey in winter, its most common uses are as follows:

- Wealthy people disposing of extra money via boat ownership
- Mosquito breeding
- Getting a fungus from rented ice skates

We've carefully considered alternative uses for this relic of a bygone era. Please check off the one you prefer, tear out this page, and mail it to your local member of Parliament.

☐ **Fill It with Garbage and Pave It Over**
Why not? There's got to be a warehouse full of Ottawa Senators 2007 Stanley Cup Champions merchandise somewhere around there.

☐ **Convert It into a Lazy Rafting River**
A hasty conversion into a leisure river for the extremely lethargic could attract tourists from as far away as Ontario towns Casselman and Arnprior.

☐ **Move All the Zebra Mussels into It**
Faced with a dangerous invasive species that threatens to destroy the delicate ecosystem of the Great Lakes, maybe we can cede the Rideau Canal to the zebra mussels and just let them live there?

☐ **Sell It on Kijiji**
A designated UNESCO Heritage Site, the Rideau Canal could fetch several thousand dollars on the popular online marketplace.

☐ **Carbonate It**
Simply by adding millions of tonnes of carbon dioxide gas, Canada could be home to the world's longest carbonated canal. Throw in some strawberry flavouring and we could have enough Clearly Canadian to quench our national thirst. The viability of turning it into a massive Orbitz reservoir needs to be studied further.

1955 Angus L. Macdonald Bridge connects Halifax and Dartmouth; suspicious Maritimers still prefer boats

Play a Game of High School Ringette

In high schools across Canada, 40% of male students and 100% of female students are subjected to at least one semester of ringette. Nationally, it is the second most popular use for a rubber ring (the most popular use cannot be described in polite company). The most recent census of Canadian ankle injuries indicates that ringette is responsible for most of them.

The official ringette handbook contains over 200 pages of rules, and while the sport has a robust presence throughout Canada, many find it cumbersome and conceptually exactly like hockey.

Stats Canada has reviewed the rules and created this handy summary of the game.

General

- Sandstorm must be played at least three times but no greater than five
- Each player must yell "Ringette!" after every goal
- Goaltenders may not ring-ding the ringer mid-ringette, unless a ring-a-ling has been called
- Each player must get a chance to play
- If someone is unable to participate in ringette they are required to cap each ringette stick after the game so nobody pokes their eye out

Safety

- Goalies are required to wear extra rings around forearms for protection
- All players must appear "totally over it"
- Be off the ice by 3 p.m. because the hockey team has a practice
- If traditional padding is unavailable, the player must wrap their limbs in standard-issue orange reflective tape
- Always spear sensibly

Ringette may have a lot of rules, but the first rule is to have fun! If you find yourself in one of Canada's large empty parking lots, why not play a game of pickup with your friends or family?

1956 Prince Edward Island returns to the spud standard

Objects Most Frequently Repurposed as Ringette Sticks

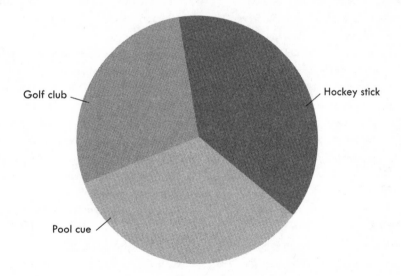

Golf club

Hockey stick

Pool cue

1957 Canadian Thanksgiving is created, replacing Canadian Sorrysgiving

Watch Canadian Television

The average Canadian spends 2.7 hours watching television per day, and despite the growing popularity of stealing American Netflix, TV remains the number one way that Canadians learn about exclusive products at Home Hardware. At first glance, visitors may be left with the impression that Canadian programming is not very different from TV in the rest of the world, but a closer viewing reveals a number of peculiarities unique to Canadian television.

SITCOMS

Canada is a well-known exporter of comedic talent, accounting for 20% of Hollywood's chuckles and nearly one-third of the guffaws. At home, the resulting shortage of quippy sidekicks, quirky neighbours, and affectionately dopey dads has meant that Canadian sitcoms have struggled to match the generation-defining heights of their American counterparts. It's a serious enough problem that many Canadians have called for a repeal of NAPTA (North American Prime Time Agreement) to protect the declining domestic sitcom industry.

SOAP OPERAS

For nearly 60 years, Canadians have been transfixed by the ongoing drama *Yonge Street*. Five nights a week, much of Canada pauses to catch up on the goings-on of an ensemble of characters living on or around the titular street in midtown Toronto. Recent plots have included:

- Brad loses his Presto card
- Nelson tells a date he's from Rosedale but he actually lives closer to Eglinton
- Amena finds a Ford Nation shirt in her laundry

REALITY TELEVISION

Canadian reality television is essentially made up of concepts "borrowed" from other countries, but with some crucial differences.

American Idol: Canada features talented young singers competing to deliver the most rousing version of Stompin' Tom's "The Hockey Song." *Big Brother: Canada* uses hidden cameras to follow the dramatic ups and downs of a group of strangers forced to survive in a house with Doug Ford shadowing their every move for four years. *Survivor: Canada*, currently in its 16th season, maroons a talented young hockey player in the remote city of Edmonton for his entire career.

NEWS PROGRAMMING

By law, national Canadian news broadcasts must include one "good news" story for every three downers. On particularly bad news days, a short video clip of a baby moose learning to walk plays in the upper corner of every major news slot. Each broadcast concludes with a 45-minute weather report, most of which is just a detailed update of snowmobile trail conditions across the country.

Local news broadcasts are usually just a voicemail from your mom describing things she saw on Facebook.

PRANK SHOWS

Perhaps the most quintessentially Canadian television genre is the "gag" show, a strange and unpleasant spectacle that forces unsuspecting people to confront unnerving scenarios for the benefit of hidden cameras. Set to a droning soundtrack and punctuated with the laughter of the damned, the gag show is a release valve for the famously polite and friendly population, allowing the nation to vicariously experience the thrill of being rude to a stranger without any of the social consequences. Many of these pranks have gotten out of hand; more than 60% of bad news stories on Canadian evening news broadcasts are reports of deaths and injuries suffered by the unlucky victims of these shows.

COMMERCIALS

Although thousands of Canadian commercials are produced every year, they all feature one of the same six actors. Unlike American TV commercials, which often have high production values and memorable characters, Canadian advertisers aim to impress the audience by demonstrating how thrifty they are. Every year, Canadian sports fans look forward to enjoying the same handful of commercials for Global's upcoming mid-season replacement shows instead of the distractingly spectacular ads that American audiences have to endure. Four out of five Canadian commercials end with very specific driving directions. As of 2017, only one Canadian TV commercial furniture pitchman has gone on to become the mayor of a major metropolis.

GAME SHOWS

One of Canada's most popular contributions to the game show oeuvre is *Supermarket Sweep*, which turned a boring weekly chore into a boring weekly program. Contestants raced each other up and down the aisles of a grocery store in a desperate quest to find the biggest, juiciest ham. The show was cancelled after several contestants tested positive for performance-enhancing coupons.

In the early 1990s, young Canadians were glued to the screens every time *Video and Arcade Top Ten* came on. The show, which featured contestants competing to beat the latest Nintendo and Sega games, combined the fun of playing video games with the dull monotony of watching somebody else hog the controller. As if that wasn't exciting enough, every episode was repeatedly interrupted by some dopey dude who counted down an arbitrary top 10 list of music videos. "Was Nicholas Picholas his real name?" is still a top 10 search term on SaskJeeves.

Top Canadian Game Show Prizes

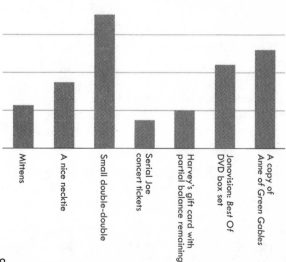

Mittens | A nice necktie | Small double-double | Serial Joe concert tickets | Harvey's gift card with partial balance remaining | Jonovision: *Best Of* DVD box set | A copy of *Anne of Green Gables*

Play the *Chopped Canada* Drinking Game

The most recent census of Canadian leisure habits indicates that 74% of Canadians prefer reality television to reality itself. Virtually all Canadian reality shows are just lower-budget versions of American reality shows with the word "Canada" added to the title. One of the most unappealing and inexplicably popular examples of this lazy reformatting of lazy television is *Chopped Canada*. Canadians everywhere love to watch chefs from around the country compete in the greatest culinary tournament import since *The Great British Bake Off*.

Host and producer Dean McDermott steals the show with his crispy tan, unintelligible commentary, and unnecessary nervous stream of softball questions, exposing McDermott as the foodie he is not.

So, the next time you settle for an episode of *Chopped Canada*, do yourself a favour and follow along with the official *Chopped Canada* drinking game.

TAKE A SWIG IF . . .
- The contestant is head chef at an airport hotel or bar
- The contestant grew up on a farm in Quebec
- The contestant got their start at the Black Hoof in Toronto

POUND A SHOT WHEN
- Dean McDermott's sweat splashes onto the judges
- A chef thickens dishes with Kraft Dinner cheese powder
- There's a close-up of a Saskatoon berry compote bubbling on the stovetop

CHUG IF . . .
- A basket item is mispronounced by Dean McDermott
- The contestant will use the prize money to buy back the family farm
- A chef overuses bacon during the dessert round

SHOTGUN A BEER IF . . .
- You went to the same high school as the contestant from Charlottetown
- A contestant deconstructs a butter tart
- Dean McDermott is deep in thought, as if he's reflecting on his adulterous past

1958 Snowmobile is invented; Canada quickly divides itself into rival Ski-Doo and Polaris gangs

Watch Canadian Netflix

Just like Stephen Harper, many Canadians enjoy spending their time watching online streaming services. Unfortunately, approximately 34% of those Canadians do not have a millennial in their household and are therefore unable to figure out how to get American Netflix—forever limited to watching whatever gets uploaded on the Canadian version. We've compiled a list of Canada's favourite TV shows and movies for your next "It's very cold so we're going to stay in and chill" Netflix night.

- 73 episodes of *Heartland*
- *Corner Gas: The Christmas Special*
- *Goon*
- *Property Brothers: After Dark*
- *Real Houseboatwives of Snout Harbour, NFLD*
- Every Ryan Reynolds movie
- *The Purge: No Apologies*
- *Gordon and Freddie*
- *Igloo of Cards*
- *Bon Cop Bad Cop Fake JFL: Gags Cop*
- Just hours of hockey fights
- *Canada's Next Top Prime Minister*
- The episode of *Degrassi* where Drake gets shot
- *Unbreakable Kim Cattrall*
- *The Hunger Games: Tim's Is Closed*
- *Law & Order: Neighbour Disputes*
- *American Horror Story: Donald Trump*
- *The West Winnipeg*
- *The Fault in the Dallas Stars*
- *Night at the ROM*

1959 Beloved actor Paul Gross is born

Attend a Canadian University

53% of Canadians aged 25 or older have completed a post-secondary education. This means that roughly half of all Canadian adults have spent four years of their life yelling, sleeping, and gaining 15 extra pounds. Even among other developed countries, Canada's rate of post-secondary enrolment is very high; it's estimated that half of all funnels sold by Canadian Tire are used for beer. More than two million Canadians are currently enrolled in a college or university program, collectively consuming 4.8 billion Pizza Pockets per year and bringing a combined 1,600 metric tonnes of laundry home to their mothers every Thanksgiving and Christmas.

Attending university is the most common way Canadians endure the frustration of watching a 70-year-old man struggle to get his PowerPoint to work.

Few experiences are more Canadian than moving to a medium-sized city 0.8 provinces away and forging friendships in the furnace of residence life that will last a lifetime.* The school you pick will change the course of your life, so choose carefully!

Dalhousie University, Halifax, NS

Located in a city whose residents treat every day like Frosh Week, "Dal," the largest school in Atlantic Canada, is famed for its hard-partying lifestyle. If you're a high school student with decent grades and you want to get far enough away from your parents that you're not obligated to come home for the second-tier holidays, Dalhousie is for you!

---

* An average of 6.3 years, or until you get sick of the baby photos they keep posting on Facebook and unfriend them.

Unique among its 180 programs:
- Donair Sauce Chemistry
- Fish Finding
- The History and Historiography of Sea Shanties

McGill University, Montreal, QC

An English-language school with two centuries of history in Montreal, McGill has high entrance standards and a reputation as the "Harvard of the North." It also has a rich athletic tradition: in earlier times, McGill students invented or helped popularize football, basketball, and ice hockey. However, a more recent effort to turn "losing a decade of your life to Montreal's swirling quicksand of cheap rent, booze, and sex" into a recognized sport has failed to find much traction. McGill offers degrees or diplomas in more than 300 fields of study, including:
- The Economics of Being Born Rich
- The Quebec Humanities (juggling, busking, LARPing)
- Ph.D. in Privilege

Carleton University, Ottawa, ON

Carleton is a commuter school made up of featureless brick buildings dedicated to creating the next generation of civil servants who will work anonymously in featureless brick buildings. Despite having one of North America's winningest sports teams, the 12-time champion Ravens men's basketball squad, Carleton undergraduates receive the most wedgies of all Canadian university students. Buildings on campus are connected by an extensive network of underground tunnels, and 60% of Carleton students would become immediately blind if exposed to natural daylight.

Among the programs offered at Carleton:

- Beige Studies
- The History of the Cubicle
- Trudeaulogy

Waterloo University, Waterloo, ON

The academic heart of "Silicon Valley North," Waterloo is well known for its engineering and computer science programs and really good free Wi-Fi. Situated not far from where RIM invented and screwed up the BlackBerry, Waterloo attracts top students who want to prepare for a lucrative career in science and technology without being bogged down by a distracting social life. Many undergraduates find it difficult to find classrooms and lecture halls because all signage is in binary. Consider these top programs:

- Have You Tried Unplugging It and Plugging It Back In?
- Surviving the Coming Robot Wars
- Cable Management (part of the fine arts program)

University of Windsor, Windsor, ON

Dangling off the exposed tip of Southern Ontario, Windsor is home to a world-class university that's famous for opening its doors to the highest percentage of foreign students and teaching them poorly. *Maclean's* consistently ranks Windsor at the bottom of its list of Canadian universities, but many say the rankings are flawed since they do not include Windsor's famously delicious pizza. Windsor offers these programs when available:

- Biohazard Diversity of the Detroit River
- Advanced Union Bargaining
- Applied Knife Crime

University of Alberta, Edmonton, AB

Originally a remote saloon where grizzled prospectors would dole out frontier wisdom in exchange for a shot of moonshine, the University of Alberta has evolved into a major research institution with more than 30,000 students. Located in the heart of Edmonton, "The Calgary of Northern Alberta," its first-year undergrads are subjected to a cruel frosh hazing ritual where they are drafted first overall by the Oilers. 80% of campus parking spaces have recently been widened to accommodate dually pickups. Choose from an extensive list of academic programs, including:

- Rodeo Broadcasting
- Cattle Massage
- Environmental Studies (three-month program, everything is fine)

Simon Fraser University, Vancouver, BC

Sandwiched between the salty ocean and the rugged coastal mountains, Simon Fraser prepares students for a lifetime of being squeezed by overwhelming forces outside their control. Well regarded for its faculties of the environment and health sciences, Simon Fraser's entrance exam requires students to hold an uncomfortable yoga position until the sun breaks through the damp morning fog or a distant whale breaches the cold and grey Salish Sea—whichever comes first! Graduates can look forward to wearing Canada's only cap made of renewable hemp and seaweed. Simon Fraser offers more than 100 undergraduate programs, including:

- Sushi Engineering
- Pre-Med (Naturopathy, Holistic Healing, and Meditation)
- Western Philosophy (west of Vernon, BC)
- Bicycle Maintenance
- Bachelor in Squatters' Rights

1960 Prime Minister Diefenbaker builds Y2K shelter

Celebrate the Canadian Holidays

Whether you're visiting your spouse's family in Canada or have been grounded at one of the country's major airports due to weather or co-pilot inebriation, you can celebrate the holidays by learning these customs.

Canadian Christmas
Canadians have been celebrating Christmas on November 25 since Canada made the switch to the Gordon Calendar in the early 2000s, though traditional Christmas is still often observed by many American and British expats.

Bathtub XXX-Mas Screech
In the Maritimes, Canadians start the holiday by whipping up a tub full of festive Christmas Screech. The drink is similar to the traditional boozy substance, with a seasonal twist of cinnamon or nutmeg, served in a copper mug.

Boxing Day
Wake up at the crack of dawn and spend the day after American Christmas standing in a LuuluuLemon line snaking around the food court, merging with the Orange Julius line.

Order the Festive Special at Swiss Chalet
Canadians everywhere look forward to enjoying a delicious bowl of Swiss Chalet's hot lemon water soup.

Hudson's Bay Holiday Window Display
Spend one to three hours gawking at windows prepared by unpaid interns.

Sexy Mall Santa
Pay a visit to Toronto's Sexy Mall Santa, who broke the Internet with his sparkling white cotton candy beard, piercing blue eyes, and the gnawing possibility that he's your new stepdad.

Call the Air Canada Customer Service Line
If you like Air Canada, you'll love re-explaining the same error to two customer service representatives and eventually escalating it to a supervisor.

1961 Your lucky penny is minted

What Canadians Look Forward to Most in the Swiss Chalet Festive Special

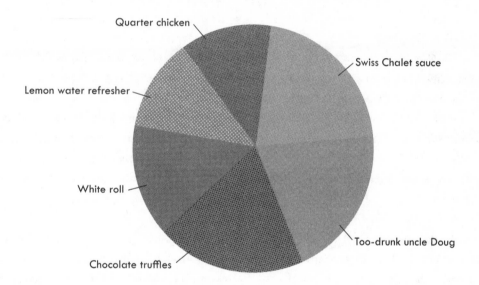

Quarter chicken

Swiss Chalet sauce

Lemon water refresher

White roll

Too-drunk uncle Doug

Chocolate truffles

1962 Zellers stores receive final renovation

Learn Canadian Baseball

Due to the Blue Jays' recent surge in popularity, more and more Canadians have been trying to learn the rules of baseball. 90% of Americans assume that it's the same game across the border and are shocked to discover several key differences:

- No stealing
- Strikes are called "give'rs," balls are called "sorrys"
- All bats have to be maple
- Catchers must wear goalie helmets and also goalie pads
- Women aren't strictly forbidden to play
- Every game ends with fireworks, but they suck

TV cameras have recently been installed in the Blue Jays stadium (formerly the SkyDome and now the Rogers Data Plan Cap Dome), introducing the Canadian version of the game to a larger audience. Viewers have been surprised to learn that, in Canada, any pitcher who records three give'rs in a row is awarded a parliamentary majority, and if the batter is hit by a pitch the offending pitcher is thrown out of the game unless the batter can convince the umpire that the pitcher is an okay guy. Foreign audiences were especially surprised to see relieving pitchers entering the game via snowmobile.

The differences do not end there. The MLB, influenced by Her Majesty's Athletics Lobby, ruled that a Canadian citizen had to be on the field every inning played on Canadian soil. American teams often have to hire a Canadian player for a three-day contract when they play the Blue Jays at home. This has led to a cottage industry of young Canadians who have to be really good at right field. Unfortunately, these players are often treated as second-class citizens and can have their roster spot revoked at any time.

Her Majesty's Athletics Lobby was the source of some controversy of late when they filed a patent for "Drinking During a Baseball Game," which would have prohibited alcohol from being sold at American MLB games. The subsequent outrage caused a player walkout, many claiming that they can't perform without being heckled by a drunk man. The dispute was settled quickly with a compromise, resulting in all American stadiums being forced to sell only American beer.

1963 First polar bear domesticated in Manitoba

What do the players think about playing in Canada? We asked some of the game's best:

"There's nothing in the rulebook that says a dog can't play."
　　　—Jean Gibbons

"The brimmed tuques are uncomfortable."
　　　—A. A. Ron

"Canada is the only place I've ever grown facial hair."
　　　—Alec Rodriguess

"The stadium here charges us for Gatorade, and none of our cell phones work!"
　　　—Anonymous

"I shave every night and wake up with a full beard every morning."
　　　—Jean Beautiste

Across the country, more and more Canadians are trying the game for themselves. Kids are trading in their lacrosse sticks for baseball sticks and their curling shoes for goose-down batting gloves. Conversations about balks and roster mechanics are happening at dinner tables around the nation. So whether you're a superfan or a good-fer-nuthin bum, at least you'll know the rules.

Did You Know?

The average Blue Jays fan throws $21.50 worth of beer on the outfield per game.

1964 Alex Trebek loses virginity

Become a Raccoon Whisperer

If you find yourself making your way home after a night on the town in Toronto, you may encounter a raccoon or two, or possibly an entire pack headed by a burly eight-kilogram gang leader, blindly bumbling towards you. Raccoon bites are the most commonly reported health incident for visitors to Toronto, followed by full-blown rabies.

For those who haven't come in contact with raccoons on a nightly basis, approaching a raccoon for the first time can be frightening. But if you follow these simple instructions you'll learn how to honourably surrender to Canada's scrappiest panda and approach every raccoon threat safely.

1. BYOB: Bring Your Own Balaclava

Balaclavas are terrifying to wear to any social gathering, and are unacceptable in all banks, most Shoppers Drug Marts, and shared spaces outside the Territories. However, should you or your family encounter nature's burglars, this terrifying tuque comes in handy: simply slip the balaclava over your head first before assisting family members with theirs, and slink past the obstructing raccoons, fooling them by becoming one of the pack.

2. U'rine Charge

Ammonia is a common repellant for raccoons. Ask whether your host or hotel carries any house urine for purchase, or prepare your own easily in any washroom. We suggest buying a travel-sized spray bottle, available at Shoppers Drug Marts nationwide, and keeping the bottle on your person, refilling when necessary.

3. Save the Leftovers

If you're coming home from a restaurant, don't forget to grab a doggy bag. Cold fries, shawarma ends, and pita scraps are all part of a complete urban raccoon diet, and can also serve as beneficial offerings should you encounter a pack lurking on your Airbnb doorstep.

1965 Canadian flag hastily thrown together night before it's due

4. Scatter

Rarely, but more often than never, you may find yourself outnumbered by rival raccoon packs engaging in an evening territorial rumble. To better your chances of survival, tell the members of your party to scatter in different directions. In a raccoon encounter of this nature, you will have a one in four chance of escaping the situation unscathed.

5. Practise Proper Handwashing

Raccoons are notoriously clean creatures—if they're around a standing body of water, they'll wash both their hands and their food. So if you're in a pinch and without any of your go-to raccoon repellant techniques, consider offering the evening beast a squirt or two of hand sanitizer for the bag of day-old bagels it's consuming in your path. If you're lucky the raccoon will gratefully accept the gift, and you may pass it safely.

6. Become Their King

Eat out of a dumpster. Turn everybody's organic waste bin upside down. Get into fights with house pets. If you act enough like a raccoon for long enough, you will gradually earn the respect of the pack. Choose your moment wisely and you'll be able to challenge the alpha raccoon to a leadership duel. If, after the ensuing tornado of claws and garbage, you emerge victorious, you will have earned yourself a loyal pack of trash monsters to do your bidding. You are a raccoon now.

1966 David Usher, Canada's Lenny Kravitz, is born in Montreal

Attend the Bordertown Olympics

In 2017, Sault Ste. Marie, Ontario, hosts the Bordertown Olympics, an international competition pitting athletes from border towns the world over against each other in a series of border town–specific events. Previously hosted in Tijuana, Buffalo, and Bratislava, this will be the first time the event will be held in Northern Ontario. It will also be the first time any major event of any kind will be held in Northern Ontario. Canada's team will be made up of athletes from the host city as well as Windsor, St. Catharines, and Abbotsford, and the event will be sponsored by the Duty Free Shop.

Book your tickets now to these marquee events:
- Rumrunning
- Competitive Underage Binge Drinking
- Customs Officer Deception
- Bridge Lineup Marathon
- Tax-Free Two-Four Deadlift
- Bridge Toll Coin Toss
- Bordertown Triathlon (River Swim, Fence Climb, Sprint Away from Homeland Security)
- Accent Mocking

Preparations for the games are already underway in the Soo, with disused ice fishing huts being converted into grandstands and the Bordertown Games Torch Pavilion being installed next to the Pee Wee Arena. Workopolis has a posting for the Bordertown Games Mascot job, a role that involves wearing six pairs of brand-new jeans at the same time and singing the Bordertown Games motto:

Place of residence? How long are you visiting? Are you bringing cash or assets worth more than $10,000 into the country?

Visitors who'll be attending the 2017 Bordertown Games should take advantage of the Total Games Experience package, which includes accommodations at the Watertower Inn, admission for two to the Sault Ste. Marie Sports Hall of Fame (in Phil Esposito's garage), and a Nexus card.

1-9-6-7 Justin Trudeau's PIN number

Diagnose Yourself with Web EhMD

In an effort to alleviate the strain on Canada's universal medical institutions, all citizens are encouraged to consult Web EhMD before visiting a clinic or emergency room. Web EhMD is the nation's fully functional disease and illness screening system, available online, through mobile web, and in the app store. Web EhMD has been a triumph, saving the provinces an average of $1.6 million in telehealth services per year.

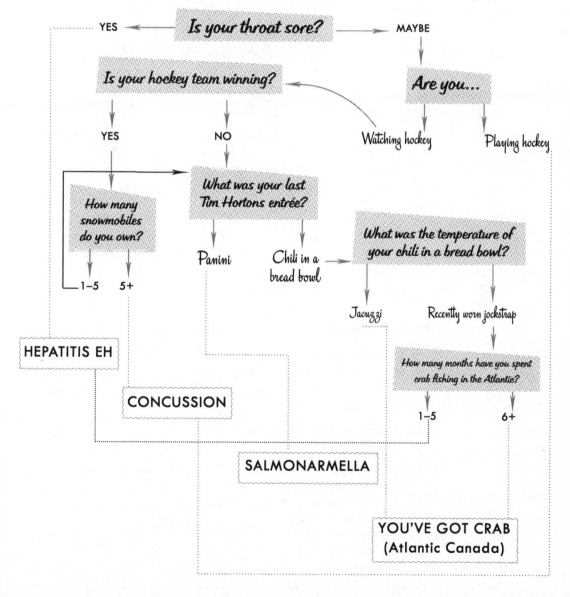

Bundle Your Services with Rogers

Saving money is easy when you bundle your services, and Rogers is passionate about helping you save money! Choose from several easy plans tailored to your media lifestyle, with a little something extra that the whole family can enjoy.

Now you can watch the game, surf the web, and call your mother crying, all at the same time!

Choose Your Cable

Whether it's hockey for Dad, *Coronation Street* for Grandma, or the Michael Bublé Christmas special for the whole family, Rogers has all your favourite channels. You won't miss a thing!

Rogers Me100
Channels include: EhMC, The Marilyn Denis Network, The Fishing News Network, +hundreds more!

Rogers Me200
Channels include: SnowTV, HGTV (Home & Gravel Television), FrancoMime, +hundreds more!

Rogers Me300
Channels include: CFL Fanzone, TUQUETV, SnowSportz, JFLplus, +hundreds more!*

Choose Your High-Speed Internet

Simply choose the channels you want, how fast you want your megabytes to fly, and where to install a phone you can't take with when you leave the house, and you're good to go with the Rog!

Speed Demon!
2.5 mbs of safe-for-work downloads, unlimited email, up to five homepages

Mainlining
4 mbs of both types of loading, unchangeable spam filter, Skypes

The Friggin Matrix
10 mbs of bits, unlimited clicking, still worse than your iPhone

---

* Sign up for a two-year contract with Rogers and receive three free months of Don Cherry's YellVision channel.

1968 Canada mentioned on *The Tonight Show with Johnny Carson*

Choose Your Phone Plan

Rogers phone bundles now come with some exciting landline options. Mobile phones are complicated, and 87% of Canadians lose them in a public bathroom. The revolutionary Rogers Home Phone eliminates 95% of the functionality and tethers it to the most important wall in your house: the kitchen wall.

French Minutes
Free outgoing calls to Quebec

French Kiss
Unlimited incoming and outgoing texts to Quebec

No surcharge for putting your lips on the phone

The Weekender
Unlimited "any time" minutes to Quebec every Saturday and Sunday

Act now and we'll throw in Rogers home security, which boasts the best protection of all the Canadian cable providers. In the event of a home invasion, our state-of-the-art system not only notifies the authorities; it also shames the burglar by finding their old Myspace page.

Money Well Spent
Customers who bundle their services are eligible for up to 5% off their total bill, helping ensure that Rogers remains one of Canada's most profitable companies.

HOW ROGERS SPENDS ITS PROFITS

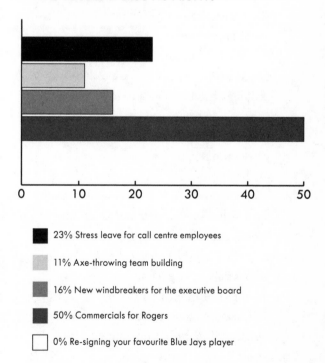

- ■ 23% Stress leave for call centre employees
- ▢ 11% Axe-throwing team building
- ▨ 16% New windbreakers for the executive board
- ■ 50% Commercials for Rogers
- □ 0% Re-signing your favourite Blue Jays player

1969 Grainstock Music Festival held in Saskatchewan

Breed a Canadian Dog

Dog breeding is the latest craze to sweep the nation. Not satisfied with the tens of thousands of existing dog breeds, Canadians have bred their companions to survive the country's bizarre extremes. From the long fur of the *Gordon Retriever* to the wheat tolerance of the *Manitoba Moosedog*, the dogs of Canada have adapted to fit their environment.

Take, for instance, the *Quebec Frenchie*, whose barks are somewhat less continental than those of French bulldogs bred in Europe. It is believed that the dogs learned this dialect to further distance themselves from other Canadian dogs.

The breeds have often come about for obvious reasons (e.g., the adorably tiny *Vancouver Apartment Dog*), but others are mysterious. No one knows how the *New Brunswick Blood Hunter* got its name, or perhaps no one has lived to tell the tale.

Canada also realizes the benefits of *not* breeding dogs and simply letting nature decide. These "mutts" often live much longer than their purebred brethren, and are extra handy around the house. They can also be found roving the countryside, searching for treats, and solving various crimes. Although they're of indeterminate breed, many locals have taken to calling them the *World's Longest Undefended Border Collies*.

It's not just creative breeding that makes a dog Canadian. The dogs share many traits with their owners, including kindness and facial hair. You'll never meet a Canadian dog that will give you bad directions or won't shake a stranger's paw. Canadian dogs are known throughout the world as good dogs, and are always shown hospitality while travelling abroad.

Breeding Canadian dogs can be a difficult endeavour, and care must be taken to determine which traits are desirable. Here's a handy guide used by top Canadian dog breeders.

Trait A	Trait B	Result
Intelligent	Long-lived	*Trebek Spaniel*
Likes car rides	Punctual	*Trenton Trucker Hound*
Trustworthy	Seaworthy	*Bluenosed Terrier*
Clumsy	Past its prime	*Our Lady Poodle*
Trusting eyes	Excellent orator	*Trudeau Shepherd*

Types of Canadian Pets

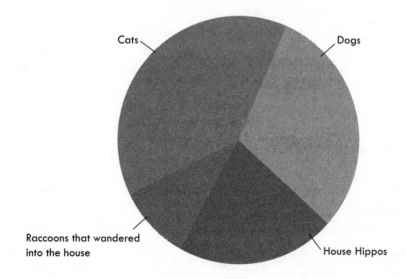

Cats

Dogs

Raccoons that wandered into the house

House Hippos

1971 Handsome son Justin Trudeau born to handsome parents

Visit British Columbia

When visiting Canada, tourists are often told to "go see British Columbia—it's heaven on earth!" This is a bold claim and far too subjective to be part of this travel guide. However, it did serve as a starting point for our statistical study of whether British Columbia is indeed "the best province" in Canada.

In order to test this, Stats Canada chose BC's five most popular visitor sites. We then logged on to tripadvisor.ca to find each site's average review score. The results were fascinating. We've included some of the most telling reviews.

STANLEY PARK, VANCOUVER—WEIGHTED AVG.: 0.3/5

Reviews

I got lost and am still lost. Please send help. 1/5

It's a great place to meet raccoons, single & ready to mingle. I'm a raccoon. 1/5

Too big. Didn't like the trees. Could have used a Tim Hortons. 2/5

OSOYOOS DESERT MODEL RAILROAD—WEIGHTED AVG.: 1/5

Reviews

I fell asleep under the model ski slope. They wouldn't give me a blanket. 1/5

Website says, "Our railroad is for kids of all ages—from 1 to 101," which is unfortunate because I was travelling with my newborn (four months) and my great-grandmother (103 years). They wouldn't let us in. 1/5

The model of the Vancouver Riots was a little distasteful. 1/5

BARKERVILLE HISTORIC TOWN AND PARK—WEIGHTED AVG.: 3/5

Reviews

The actors took their roles a little too seriously. One man hadn't showered in two months. Another tried stealing my boots. 2/5

Nothing was made of gold. 1/5

I got a mesh-back trucker hat at the gift store! 5/5

1972 Canada ends Cold War

GARBAGE DUMP IN SURREY—WEIGHTED AVG.: 4.5/5

Reviews

Great place to find needles when you're in a bind. 4/5

The bears. Oh lord! The bears. My dear, poor Richard is gone. 1/5

Pretty nice B&B for the price. 4/5

TRIPP KEELER'S GROW OP (LOCATION NOT REVEALED BY OWNER)—WEIGHTED AVG.: 1/5

Reviews

The raid wasn't cool, man. I'm in jail for seven years now. Bummer. 2/5

Wait. What? 1/5

Tripp's a rad dude. I'd chill with him any day. 3/5

TOTAL AVG. FOR BRITISH COLUMBIA: 0.4/5

Canada's national average from all tripadvisor.ca reviews is around 2/5. Given how low British Columbia scored, Stats Canada is placing this province under a travel advisory. If you do choose to visit British Columbia, here are the top activities in which to partake while exploring Canada's easternleast province:

- Buy day pass for whale watching—see no whales
- Save enough money to visit Whistler for half a day (no skiing—too expensive)
- Take a selfie in Tofino while wearing a wetsuit and tell your coworkers, every chance you get, that you know how to surf
- Forget to pack your rain gear and have your entire two-week vacation ruined
- Explore your inner self with BC's finest Kush
- Discover ancient "cave paintings" deep in East Vancouver's alleyways
- Get eaten by a bear
- Try to meet all nine people living in northern British Columbia
- Shop at BC's largest mall, Metropolis at Metrotown, and enjoy a cold-cut trio from Subway
- Forsake all non-essential personal belongings and begin your journey from Vancouver to Bear Camp. Run out of food in Prince Rupert. Continue hike until death. Wait peacefully in eternal rest until your body is discovered 20 years later by more skilled hikers

Buy a House in Vancouver

Congratulations! You're thinking of buying a house, something only 12% of Canadians will ever accomplish in their lifetimes. Reverse Congratulations! You're buying a house in Vancouver. According to the most recent census, all homeowners in Vancouver either play for the Canucks or are families of 25 living in three bedrooms.

Fear not, Stats Canada has compiled these steps to owning your Vancouver home.

Step One: Hope Your Great-Aunt Dorothy Passes On and Leaves Her House to You

The family is well aware that Dorothy doesn't have many solid years left. You'd better get in there quick and butter her up before the dementia sets in. If you wait too long, Dorothy won't be found to be "sound of mind," making new revisions to her will void and your future house a mere dream.

Step Two: Buy a P.O. Box in Downtown Vancouver and Tell People You Live There

A very realistic goal. P.O. boxes are cheap, plus your friends will consider you 72% more impressive if your mailing address starts with V6B. VERY IMPORTANT: DO NOT ACTUALLY MOVE INTO P.O. BOX. You cannot afford this. Instead, live in one of the many suburbs of the suburbs of Vancouver, or a garbage dump. Either will suffice.

Step Three: Move to Vancouver, Washington

Vancouver's sister city to the south has many of the same features that make Vancouver, BC, so appealing: a damp and miserable climate, proximity to nature that you'll never take advantage of, and vegans! Thanks to America's descent into populist fear-mongering and economic uncertainty, houses have never been cheaper.

We truly hope you find a place to call home in Vancouver. However, if this plan doesn't work, you can always move to New Brunswick.

1973 Roots, Canada's most successful sweatpants company, is founded by two draft dodgers

Unlock the Hidden Pub in Gastown, BC

Exit Stadium-Chinatown Station and head up and to the left past the old woman wearing a bowler cap. This street should look familiar—it's West Cordova! You've been here before; make your way down as if you're intending to score some crank, but instead hang a left through the Community Thrift & Vintage. Ignore the elderly shop-keep and run straight through the back. You emerge in Blood Alley Square. To crack this befuddling puzzle, simply go up, left, down, and left, repeatedly. You will end up at the same location until you hear the charmed whistle of a nearby vagabond, at which point you'll finally be someplace that looks different.

Go through the revealed entrance and proceed north to ditch Blood Alley. Do not be spooked! You have arrived at a neighbourhood Needle Exchange. Follow the signs labelled "Methadone," head right, up one flight, and right once more. A couple of enemies will impede your progress, but do not engage. Ignore them and continue on your path. At the fork in the hall, keep right to the end. Leap safely through the window into a pile of trash. Finally, go right.

If you've followed the directions carefully, you will see two tacky statues of cowboys. Take the hidden entrance at the base of the one on the left. You've reached Moxie's Grill & Bar.

1974 Bachman and Turner take care of all Canadian business

Grow Old in Canada

Nearly 25% of Canada's population are senior citizens, and that number is expected to grow significantly over the next few decades. Fortunately, the quality of Canadian eldercare has improved by leaps and bounds in the last 1.5 centuries. Viking funerals, ice floe vacations, and the New Brunswick blood ceremony have faded from memory, replaced with advanced medicine, palliative care, and simply being nicer to Grandpa.

As your parents and their weird friends enter their twilight years, older citizens are expected to wield an even bigger influence on Canadian society. The elderly's propensity for heading to the polls has earned them increased clout in the political realm, giving them access to care their grandchildren could only dream of. Initiatives such as Meals on Wheels, affordable nursing homes, and the Free Ferrari Program are the government's way of giving back to the greatest generation to volunteer for Elections Canada. These perks and more make it easier for the elderly to not only survive, but thrive.

Seniors have been perceived as a drain on the country's healthcare system, but research has shown that their average medical bill has plummeted over the last generation. Unless doctors are suddenly charging less for colonoscopies, this means that the elderly are getting less sick. Perhaps it's all the old-country cooking or the shopping mall exercise, but some suggest it's something different entirely.

Rumour has it that a secret cabal of elderly meet periodically to determine the fate of the country. Yes, everyone suspects that rich old people control everything already, but this is different. They're not particularly rich and they might be someone you know. Sources say they meet at the local Tim Hortons at 7 a.m. to discuss their plans to manipulate the democratic system. Representatives of this cabal are said to have Parliament Hill on speed dial, though they often have difficulty finding the speed dial function on their new phone and they wish their granddaughter would be a bit more patient when they ask for her help.

Who are these powerful, connected, extremely slow-driving "Elderlites"?

Canada's seniors are actually growing stronger instead of sicker. Gone are the days of the "sandwich generation," where your aging parents eventually become a burden just when you're raising your own family. Unyouthful citizens are maintaining their driver's licences longer, Sears will still sell them clothes, and their sex drives are in full bloom! Today's wrinkleds are also living at home much longer, enjoying their paid-off houses and rejecting advice from their children that "they should really Airbnb all those spare bedrooms." What are they doing in those big empty homes? Nobody knows. According to leading home security companies, it's senior citizens who own the most protected residences. If you're not in the will, there's no way you're getting in!

This demographic elderwave has not come without its problems. With so many citizens defying nature's will, some provinces have considered reintroducing the Viking funeral. Wild coyotes have been allowed to roam within city limits for just a little longer than before. The informational pamphlet "It's Time to Go" has been spotted in many Talbot's locations. Members of Canada's Fifth-Greatest Generation are said to feel threatened by the young prime minister's boyish body, worrying that it could signal the beginning of a slow shift away from policies that favour the needs of old rich white people over all others. As this book goes to press, Canada's Silver League is debating which obsolete and vaguely racist expressions to keep in their vocabulary.

Despite these recent changes, it still pays to be old nowadays. After the baby boomers trigger the inevitable global economic collapse, seniors will be the only ones who know how to grow food, make sweaters, or run a decent book club. In the meantime, perhaps we can learn something from super-old people. It may save our lives, and theirs.*

---

* Through experimental technology that replaces their blood with blood of the young, extending their lifespans in an ungodly battle against nature.

Census of the Elderly

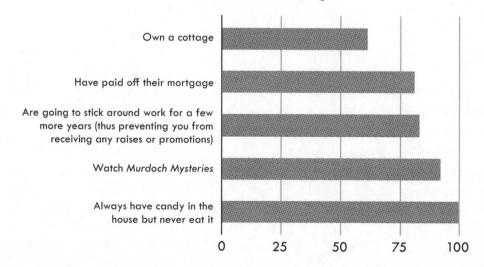

Visit the Property Brothers' First Flip

If you find yourself in the Ranchtowne district of beautiful Maple Ridge, British Columbia, you might want to drop in at the Property Brothers' treehouse, completely reconstructed by twins Jonathan and Drew Scott back in 1988. At the age of 10, the pair kindled their brotherly love for house-flipping, taking on their very first renovation and becoming the youngest twin house mutilators in Canadian history.

Located in Vancouver Lite, a mere 50 kilometres from the hustle and bustle of downtown Van City, the treehouse has unrestricted views of the surrounding mountains. A nature lover's dream and a stone's throw from Golden Ears Provincial Park, the space touts a total living area of over six rectangular metres, two-thirds of which are high-quality laminate hardwood flooring, complementing the rich and retro knotted pine cabinets and trimming throughout.

A number of fixtures have been swapped for environmentally friendly appliances, in addition to the various recycled materials used to build the clubhouse. While many have called the move industrious, the Property Brothers suffered a PR nightmare after replacing the windows with 60% recycled glass from a local needle exchange program.

Features

- Juice box cellar
- 3/4 washroom with composting toilet
- Recycling bin locks
- Comic book dehumidifier
- Snack cubby

Renophiles rejoice! Drop by the Scott brothers' clubhouse between Tuesday and Thursday and receive a personal guided tour from eldest brother and *All-American Amusement Parks* host JD Scott, who occasionally appears on the Property Brothers' programs as various handymen delivering bad news about black mould.

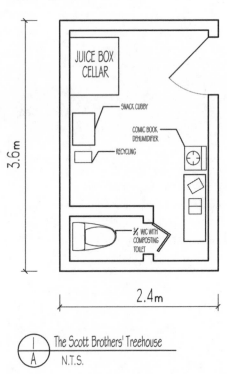

The Scott Brothers' Treehouse
N.T.S.

Enjoy Canada's Greatest Resource: Dipping Sauce

More than 20% of the world's freshwater reserves lie within Canadian borders, a fact that may become more important as the effects of climate change and salty snacks force more Americans to look north for a quencher. From the emerald-green glacial lakes of the Rockies to the roaring rivers feeding the St. Lawrence, the Canadian landscape is defined by these important sources of water.

Less well known, however, is the fact that Canada also controls 100% of the world's Swiss Chalet Dipping Sauce supply. Deep under the arctic permafrost, enormous underground gravy reservoirs are kept warm by active tectonic motion. Although the sauce does naturally bubble to the surface in a few remote locations, most of what Canadians consume is extracted through sauce pumps or dug from the ground in areas where the sauce has mixed with the loose earth to form a substance called "saucesand." The thirst for sauce has shaped Canadian society, with many Maritimers relocating to the sauce-producing West when Canadian tastes shifted away from cod and towards rotisserie chicken.

After being pulled from the earth, the crude sauce is shipped to enormous sauce refinement centres where herbs and spices are mixed in to create the final product. The sauce is then transported by train to the major sauce consumption centres in the south. The demand is so great that several of the largest sauce refiners, such as Saucecor and Imperial Gravy, have proposed the construction of massive and controversial pipelines to bring the sauce to market more quickly. Justin Trudeau's continued reluctance to support the St. Hubert East project may cost him votes next election, but the anti-sauce lobby has been very effective in rallying public opposition to the sauce pipes, citing disasters like the 2009 leak that turned Lake Nipigon into a thick and delicious bowl of flavour.

Even though most Canadians recognize the environmental risks associated with the production and transport of dipping sauce, consumption continues to increase every year. Coupled with declining reserves, this demand has pushed the cost of "brown gold" to record highs on the Toronto Condiment Commodity Exchange; sauce speculation is now threatening to upend the Canadian economy. There's great pressure to create a dipping sauce alternative, but the options discovered so far (mushroom sauce, Jackson-Triggs red wine reduction sauce, expired French's ketchup) have failed to catch on with Canadian diners.

Even if Canada's thirst for sauce can be curbed, trouble may lurk on the horizon: more than half of Canada's freshwater is used to fill those little bowls of lemon water you're supposed to dip your fingers into.

1976 Montreal Olympics bankrupt surrounding area

Become Prime Minister

After Drake's personal stylist and the guy who travels everywhere with the Stanley Cup, the prime minister is the most powerful figure in Canada. Reporting only to the Queen via a random person representing her because she's already got a lot on her plate, the prime minister presides over Parliament, directs the passage of new laws, and commands the full might of the Canadian military (excluding the covert attack-bear program—they went rogue). A tireless job requiring long, lonely hours and exposing whoever holds it to the scrutiny of the public, the calling has been answered by a mere 23 individuals over the last century and a half.

Who are our prime ministers? It's a list as diverse as our great nation.

White:

100%

Men:

95%

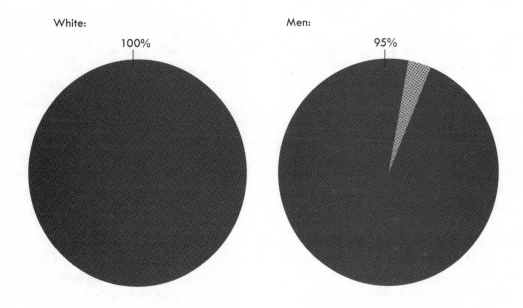

While the average Canadian can name only a handful ("Trudeau, New Trudeau, Sweater Guy, Chrétien . . . uh . . . Maloney?"), every PM has etched their own mark on our nation's history:

Alexander Mackenzie (1873–1878): Eliminated high tariffs on imported luxuries like itchy blankets and soap

Sir Robert Borden (1911–1920): Famously humiliated Wilfrid Laurier in the House of Commons by declaring, "He who smelt it is most certainly the one who hath dealt it!"

Arthur Meighen (1926–a bit later in 1926): First PM with silent letter in surname

John Diefenbaker (1957–1963): Enacted short-lived law making men's hats mandatory

Lester B. Pearson (1963–1968): Introduced new Canadian flag, replacing controversial previous flag featuring cartoon image of Queen Victoria consuming banquet of Canada's natural resources

Unlike the American political system, where citizens go to the polls to directly elect their leaders every fourth November, Canada's prime minister is the leader of the party* whose members of Parliament† win the most ridings‡ during an election that can be called every year, or two, or basically at any point through some sort of constitutional mechanics that few people understand. There are no term limits in Canada, so it is therefore possible that a prime minister could lead the country forever, trapped in limbo between life and death, presiding over an infinite number of parliamentary sessions until time itself warps and distorts into a Möbius strip of endless public service. However, we usually get sick of most governments before that can happen.

Canadian election campaigns are typically brief, usually less than three months or ten Edmonton Oilers wins, whatever comes first.

---

* A group of like-minded public servants who prefer the same coloured ties.

† Nine local representatives with deep connections to the region or 20-somethings who filled out a form online.

‡ Arbitrarily subdivided chunks of land.

1978 Guy who drives a Trans Am bullies your dad →

Become Prime Minister (continued)

Campaigning: By the Numbers

Kiss 812 babies (64% cute, 36% not cute)

Spend five days campaigning in Southern Ontario for every hour spent campaigning in Northern Ontario

Wear nine pairs of jeans and six plaid shirts while meeting with Western farmers

Eat 2.4 kilograms of cheese while campaigning in Quebec

Spend 416 minutes delivering speeches saying that oil pipelines are bad

Spend 501 minutes delivering speeches saying that oil pipelines are good

Expose a total of 4.4 metres of bare forearm skin (cumulatively) while rolling up sleeves in Ontario automotive factories

Smile through gritted teeth during 11.2 hours of Celtic music in Nova Scotia

Make 1,911 empty promises

Do you want to become prime minister? It could happen! In rare cases when a leader cannot be chosen at a party leadership convention, the Constitution allows for the party to select their leader from the general population. The law provides three options:

- Arrange all Canadians in a line from shortest to tallest and pick the person in the middle
- Require all Canadians to answer a skill-testing question including multiplication and division
- Distribute 34 million coffee cups—one of them with "YOU ARE THE NEW PRIME MINISTER" printed under the rim

If you actually become the prime minister, you can expect a handful of exclusive perks. The PM's family gets to live at 24 Sussex Drive, a beautiful heritage-designated home that is mostly not haunted. The PM also gets added to the iMessage Group Chat with the other leaders of G7 nations. And finally, as leader of Canada, you will receive a comprehensive healthcare plan, identical to every other Canadian's. Unless you decide to repeal that.

1979 First Polkaroo successfully bred in captivity

Things That Are Older Than Justin Trudeau

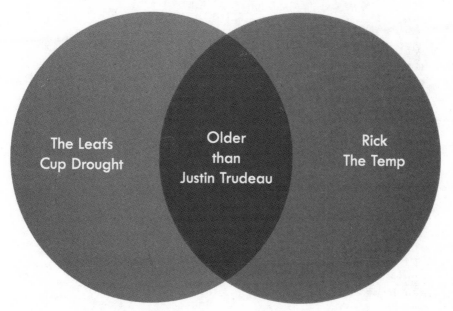

The Leafs
Cup Drought

Older
than
Justin Trudeau

Rick
The Temp

1980 *Saturday Night Live* imports more Canadians

Memorize the Prime Ministers

A baby born in Canada has a 0.000002% chance of becoming prime minister, which is actually higher than the odds of winning Lotto 6/49, arriving at your destination ahead of schedule when travelling via the Edmonton Transit System, or this video being available in your region.

All good Canadians can list every prime minister in order, and they're required to do so whenever they renew their passport, are pulled over for speeding, or try to return produce to a grocery store. According to the most recent census of elementary school students, memorizing the list of Canadian prime ministers is the third most common source of classroom stress, after writing q's in cursive and memorizing "I need to go to the bathroom" in French. Here's a handy mnemonic.

Sir John A. Macdonald	Many
Alexander Mackenzie	Men
Sir John A. Macdonald	Made
Sir John Abbott	Attempts
Sir John Thompson	To
Sir Mackenzie Bowell	Become
Sir Charles Tupper	The
Sir Wilfrid Laurier	Leader
Sir Robert Borden	But
Arthur Meighen	Most
William Lyon Mackenzie King	Merely
Arthur Meighen	Made
William Lyon Mackenzie King	Many
R. B. Bennett	Bumbling
William Lyon Mackenzie King	Mistakes
Louis St. Laurent	Losing
John Diefenbaker	Decisively
Lester B. Pearson	Persistently
Pierre Trudeau	The
Joe Clark	Candidates
Pierre Trudeau	That
John Turner	Triumph
Brian Mulroney	Make
Kim Campbell	Canadian
Jean Chrétien	Citizens
Paul Martin	More
Stephen Harper	Heavily
Justin Trudeau	Taxed

1981 Triumph releases their best album

168

Get Yourself a Custom NHL Jersey

Canadians love to show their support for their favoured NHL team by displaying that logo everywhere—as their Twitter avatar, across thousands of dollars of merchandise in their man cave, as a shoddy tattoo they received at a friend's bachelor party—and by wearing the team's jersey on their back. Many Canadians take it a step further and get customized NHL jerseys celebrating either their own last name or a funny inside joke that only their team's fan base will understand; ultimately, they'll take an old jersey and tape a new name over the name of a player who's been traded away.

NHL Jersey Sales

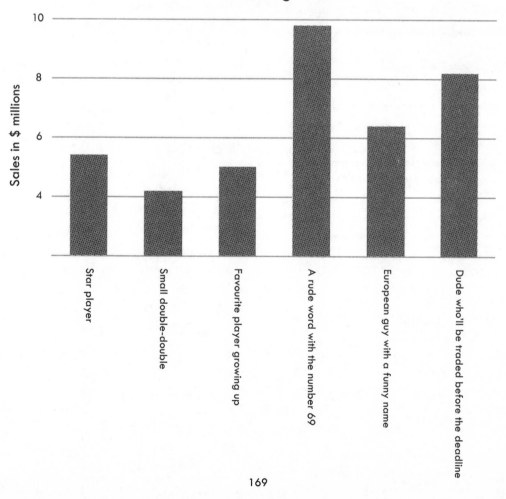

Host a Canadian Dinner Party

The average Canadian eats one "dinner" per day. The calories consumed during a Canadian dinner can be crucial for staying warm, lifting a canoe over your head, or rioting after a southern expansion team beats your favourite team in the first round of the playoffs. However, a Canadian dinner can be many things; our research has identified a variety of meals common to different parts of the country:

- Ontario: Slightly burnt Tim Hortons panini eaten while driving down the 401
- Newfoundland: A cheesecloth sack of rubbery meat and vegetables downed out of polite respect for your mother
- Yukon: Whatever can be wrestled away from the snapping jaws of a wolf
- British Columbia: A single shot of wheatgrass juice
- New Brunswick: A lavish banquet piled high with the season's harvest, attended by your closest allies and your most mortal enemy

Planning to invite some Canadians over for dinner? No matter which coast or inland backwater your guests come from, we have some surefire tips to guarantee that your next Canadian dinner party is a success:

- DO mail the invitations early, accommodating Canada Post's tendency to "wait until the moon is right" before delivering your mail
- DO steal a whole bunch of napkins from Tim's ahead of time
- DO use the back deck as a second fridge
- DO start cooking early; the puck drops at 7:30
- DON'T invite Becky

Seating

For groups less than eight, allow your guests to seat themselves. For larger dinner parties, consider seating arrangements that would separate guests with potentially conflicting views, such as Liberals and Conservatives, Oilers and Flames fans, or people for or against Drake's beard.

Setting the Table

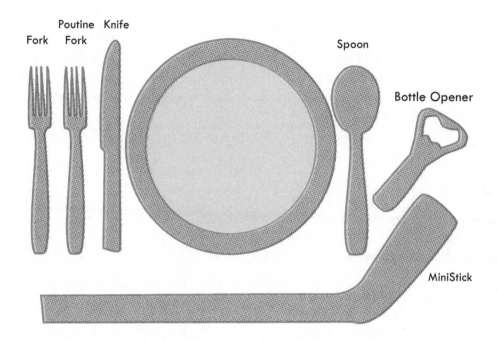

Fork   Poutine   Knife   Spoon   Bottle Opener   MiniStick

Conversation

A great Canadian dinner party should feature some lively conversation. Ideally you should stick to topics universal to all Canadians and unlikely to offend anybody. Below are some questions and conversation starters you may want to use:

- Did you ever have an indoor recess because there was a bear in the schoolyard?
- Ian Hanomansing: total dreamboat, right?
- Tell us about your favourite fishing rod
- Who would you rather: Alice Munro or Margaret Atwood?
- What Tragically Hip song was playing when you saw your father cry for the first time?
- The year Grandpa got lost in the blizzard
- Do tell us about your totally unique tattoo and the meaning behind it
- Canada's creepiest PMs

Learn the Origins of Canadian Place Names

From Spuzzum, BC, to Climax, NL, Canada is home to many proud towns with strange names. You don't get to choose where you were born, but the residents of Urin, SK, probably wish they could! Most Canadians do not live in a place that sounds like a bodily function, but even some of the more familiar cities and towns across Canada earned their names in surprising ways:

Oshawa, Ontario: An old Iroquois word meaning "land where the pickup trucks have 'No Fear' decals."

Montreal, Quebec: Montreal takes its name from the nearby peak, Mount Bunch of Royal Nerds Up There LARPing All Day.

Regina, Saskatchewan: Formerly Fort Assiniboia, the city's name was changed to honour the 1981 official visit by the host of *Jonovision America:* Regis Philbin.

Calgary, Alberta: A misspelling of "Cow Area."

London, Ontario: Thought to be named after the English capital, this Ontario city is actually named after the Warren Zevon song about werewolves.

Saskatoon, Saskatchewan: Obviously something to do with a sasquatch cartoon.

Wawa, Ontario: Named after the mournful cries of hitchhikers who get stuck there.

Dawson City, Yukon: Home to the world's largest *Dawson's Creek* fan fest, the city officially changed its name from Alf City in 1999.

Truro, Nova Scotia: Named after the sound a dog makes if you try to train it to say "Trudeau."

White Rock, British Columbia: A tribute to the genre of music enjoyed by most local residents.

Place Names

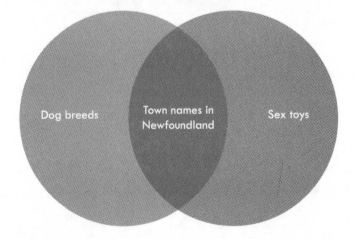

Dog breeds   Town names in Newfoundland   Sex toys

Celebrate Canadian Thanksgiving

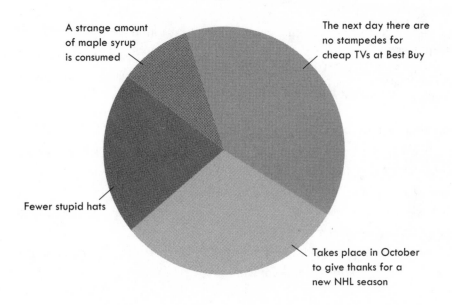

A strange amount of maple syrup is consumed

The next day there are no stampedes for cheap TVs at Best Buy

Fewer stupid hats

Takes place in October to give thanks for a new NHL season

1982 First time Leafs trade away all young prospects in exchange for aging veteran of limited value

Observe Canadian Law

Canadians are generally a law-abiding people; 77% of inmates in Canadian prisons are there as a result of library book infractions. While many Canadian disputes are settled extra-legally through mediation processes such as the Truth and Reconciliation Tractor Pull, the Criminal Code of Canada does include a number of laws that must be respected:

- Illegal to sell an alcoholic drink without a spicy garnish
- The Lowest Price Is the Law: all stores in Canada are required to honour the price of any competitor
- Illegal to select an American forward in the first round of any fantasy hockey draft
- Aboriginal issues must be ignored in both official languages
- If caught smuggling Kinder Surprises over the border, the guilty party must pay $100 in fines and listen to one Nickelback album
- Foreign purchasers of snowmobiles must remit a 15% additional sales tax
- The word "Fabricland" must be immediately followed with a louder and more insistent "FABRICLAND!"
- Illegal to mix Blue Jays merchandise with Expos merchandise
- Must keep a CD copy of at least one *Big Shiny Tunes* compilation album in your glove box (but number 2 is the best)
- Canadians must purchase mattresses from Sleep Country Canada and it is illegal to buy a mattress from anywhere else

See a Cover Band

Average Canadians are workin' for the weekend. According to the most recent census of working-class revellers, when the weekend finally rolls around they plan on crackin' 6.7 brews and getting loose to the sounds of a cover band.

Given the punishingly long distances between major cities and the stringent work-visa rules restricting the length of roadie ponytails, many major music acts do not tour in Canada. Closer to home, as soon as Canadian acts find an audience abroad, they take the first Bublé train out of town. And so to satisfy the nation's legendary thirst for workmanlike blues-rock chug, a thriving cover band industry has evolved to fill the gap. From the coziest East Coast legion halls to the most hallowed Prairie legion halls to the trendiest West Coast legion halls, you can count on finding a cover band performing wherever the number of people in the audience is equal to or greater than the number of amps on stage.

Highest Grossing Canadian Cover Bands
- Bachman Turner Underdrive
- Australian Nickelback
- Rage Against the Poutine
- Mostly Dressed Ladies
- "Shania" Live
- Four of the Members of Broken Social Scene Play the Hits!
- Timbit McGraw
- The Sk8er Bois
- Elton Jean
- Matthew Just Okay Band
- All Nude Our Lady Peace Experience
- Carly and the Jepheads
- Fat Drake
- The April Winos
- Crosby, Staal, Nash & Yzerman

1984 Moustaches reach apex in hockey fashion

Become a Billionaire

In addition to controlling 99% of the country's maple syrup supply, Canada's richest 1% has a major influence on the Canadian economy and society as a whole. While the average annual household income is 76,000 Canadian dollars (or 840 Canadian Tire dollars), a small handful of Canadian individuals belong to the elite company of Canadian billionaires. Who are they and how did they acquire such incredible wealth?

The Thomson Family

Scions of a media empire founded by Roy Thomson, 1st Baron Thomson of Fleet. Roy got his start selling radios in Toronto in the 1930s, back when the earliest Rush songs were just beginning to be played on local stations. After amassing great wealth as publishers of a number of British newspapers, the Thomsons expanded into television, financial services, and hoarding the hockey cards your mom brought to Goodwill. The current chairman of the corporation is David Thomson, ranked among the top 20 richest people on the planet. He is said to be so wealthy that he doesn't even bother switching to Wi-Fi when streaming things on his phone.

Galen Weston Jr.

Known to Canadians as "The Notorious GWJ," Weston Jr. is the chairman of Loblaw Companies Ltd., which controls virtually the entire country's winter access to fresh fruits and vegetables. His frequent appearance in commercials for the Loblaws brand has meant that 54% of Canadians report having experienced at least one awkward sex dream involving him. And given his political connections (he was Stephen Harper's senior sweater adviser), some have speculated that Weston Jr. may one day run for office; if successful, that would mean an expensive rebranding of many Loblaws products as "Prime Minister's Choice."

The Scrap King of Hamilton

A familiar sight around Burlington Street, Dougie the Scrap King has amassed enormous wealth and power one old barbecue at a time. Don't be deceived by his facial sores, rusty shopping cart full of copper wire, and discarded tinfoil Stanley Cup replicas. Dougie has turned your trash to his treasure and currently ranks among the richest people in the nation.

Snow

After scoring his one and only international hit in 1993, Snow invested his "Informer" earnings wisely. Snow, who is 0% Jamaican, diversified his investments and carefully managed the risk to his portfolio. Great wealth has not changed Snow; he lives modestly and continues to speak in a ridiculous Caribbean patois. According to our most recent census, he owns Canada's largest collection of round wire-rim glasses.

Arthur Irving

Born into a family of East Coast entrepreneurs and industrialists, Arthur Irving presides over a group of companies in the logging, transportation, and energy sectors. The Irving companies touch every aspect of Canadian life, from the fuel that powers the train bringing your crappy coffee to your town, to the train itself, to the pulp that becomes the paper cup that holds the coffee that you throw in the snowbank. Irving hasn't let his success affect him; he still changes his own oil and spends much of his time pursuing his hobby: building massive oil tankers.

The McCain Family

Founders of McCain Foods Ltd., the potato kings and queens of Canada, the McCains have built an empire on spuds. 84% of Canadians eat at least one McCain potato every day, and it's believed that the Canadian economy would sputter to a halt within six days of an interruption to the McCain potato supply. An attempt by the McCain family to acquire a cheese factory was blocked after the government enacted the country's strong poutine antitrust laws. Even without curds, three generations of McCains have turned carbs to cash, keeping their potato-growing techniques a secret for decades. But one of McCain's trade secrets may have been revealed, as the company was recently sued by Environment Canada for buttering their soil.

Your Vancouver Landlord

A recent addition to the list of Canadian billionaires, your Vancouver landlord is now one of the wealthiest Canadians, and getting wealthier every month. In exchange for 440 square feet of Kitsilano to call your own, your Vancouver landlord siphons more than three-quarters of your monthly salary (plus utilities) and spends only 4% of it on maintenance and repairs. Your Vancouver landlord has recently maximized further profits by adding several illegal suites to properties and refusing to return your damage deposit because of some chipped paint you didn't notice when you moved in. Next year, your Vancouver landlord is expected to pursue a new investment opportunity: kicking everybody out and renting your apartment as an Airbnb for $300 per day.

1986 David Suzuki's urine-powered car suppressed by federal government

Play Toronto Maple Leafs Bingo

B	I	N	G	O
Blame it on Dave Nonis	Truculence	"We're only one or two pieces away from being a contender"	"Just one Cup before I die"	Blame it on the goaltending
The Battle of Ontario means nothing now	Celebration for a Cup-winning team from before colour photographs existed	Rebuilding year	Empty seats at the ACC at the start of periods	"Yeah, but we got Auston Matthews"
"We just need guys who play like Wendel Clark"	"This is our year"	Free reference to all the Stanley Cups the Leafs have won	50 Mission Cap	Unrelenting media drives another star player out of town
Mike Babcock	"Start planning the parade"	"At least we're not Edmonton"	Awesome start to the season, tails off in November	Wayne Gretzky's high stick no-call on Doug Gilmour
Blame it on a European player	May 13, 2013	Reference to the Shanaplan	"Remember the '02 Conference Final?"	Blame it on Harold Ballard

1987 "O Canada" rewritten to include more synth →

Visit the Newfoundland Iceberg Museum

Newfoundland and Labrador is home to a storied history, beautiful landscapes, and a shitload of frozen ice chunks. All along the 29,000 kilometres of coastline, towns decimated by the decline of the fish stocks try to find ways to attract tourists.

One of the least successful attempts was the Newfoundland Iceberg Museum in Gander. Built entirely from ice chiselled off icebergs, the museum operated for only six months—no one had thought about how to keep it cool in the summertime. Taxpayers were outraged by the steep 10% levy placed on Newfoundland's favourite vice (14 beers) used to fund this monument to Maritime hubris. The failed museum joined the ranks of other failed Canadian tourist attractions, such as the Hamilton Museum of Science and Smog, the Lloydminster Daylight Savings Interpretive Centre, and the Gatineau Musée des Beaux-Arts et Fromages Fins.

OTHER CONTROVERSIES THAT PLAGUED THE MUSEUM

- An exhibit celebrating the iceberg that sunk the *Titanic*. Many deemed this to be "inappropriate," "tasteless," and "How dare you? People lost their lives. Show some respect."
- Stray dogs would come to the museum and pee on the ice walls, forcing the museum to launch a "Don't Eat the Yellow Snow" ad campaign aimed at children, which ultimately deterred parents from visiting.
- The museum tried to get the CBC to cover its opening, but the network thought this was a joke and sent a correspondent from *This Hour Has 22 Minutes*. Unfortunately, 23% of Canadian tourists still think this was just an awesome Mary Walsh segment and not an actual taxpayer-funded museum.

Although the museum ultimately melted and flooded all buildings within a one-kilometre radius, the curators did not give up hope. They've roped off the main puddle area where it once stood, and for a greatly reduced fee, visitors can come to the site and learn about the history of the museum. Additionally, the museum now hosts polar bear swims in the puddle. It's also become one of the town's most popular places for ne'er-do-wells to come and throw rocks in the water.

1988 First tear shed at Blue Rodeo concert

Dress Like a Canadian

Canadians are a simple people when it comes to fashion. 95% of clothes in Canada are made from denim, flannel, or whatever they make hockey pants out of. Fortunately, this has led to a lot of inspiring choices when it comes to crafting those outfits.

CANADIAN TUXEDO: The Canadian Tuxedo is a broad term that simply refers to any time a very fashionable person pairs a denim jacket with a pair of jeans. It is the most popular outfit choice for weddings, barn parties, weddings in a barn, a night out at the bar, your cousin's funeral, Canadian Thanksgiving, when a new prime minister is sworn in, when the tides change, and when summoned before the governor general to be awarded the Order of Canada. Alternatively, try pairing jeans with a denim vest for a more casual look.

What Kinds of Plaid do Canadians Have?

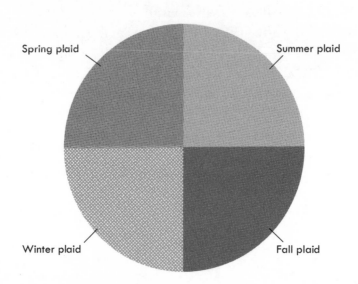

Spring plaid

Summer plaid

Winter plaid

Fall plaid

FLANNEL: 99% of Canadians have seasonal plaid patterns. In fact, in Canada the words "solstice" and "equinox" are synonymous with putting away their outgoing plaid and donning a fresh set of seasonally appropriate flannels. Canadians love flannel plaid because it's cozy and warm but also because it works for all the major Canadian subcultures: bro, lumberjack, lesbian, lesbian lumberjack, when politicians want to appear easygoing and relatable, Nirvana cover band, and as a dress shirt.

TUQUE: The tuque has become a staple of any Canadian outfit due to its ability to keep ears warm and hide a bad hair day. 32% of Canadians are unable to spell "tuque" correctly but own at least four.

HOCKEY JERSEY: Excluding jerseys worn by actual players during actual NHL games, 99% of the world's hockey jerseys are worn by Canadians. The other 1% are worn by Kevin Smith (who gets bonus Canadian points for pairing it with a pair of denim shorts).

Where Do Canadians Get Their Clothes?

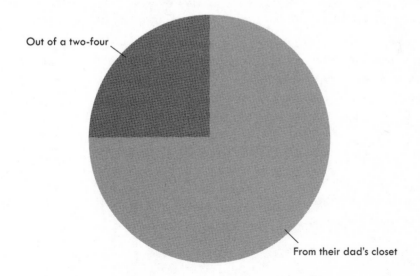

Out of a two-four

From their dad's closet

SAVE THE VILLAGE FROM THE
WHITE WITCH OF SASKATOON

In the quaint hamlet of Cathedral Bluffs, the legend of the White Witch of Saskatoon has haunted villagers for centuries. She's feared by dogs, schoolchildren, and the elderly; the mere mention of her late at night can weaken the bowels of the bravest. Tales of her appearance range from a beautiful woman to an old decrepit bag lady to a shapeshifter hell-bent on kidnapping the village children to feed to her pet wolves. 97% of Saskatchewan residents believe they are feeling her presence when they suddenly get a swift chill on a warm summer day. Often blamed for the spoiled autumn harvest, she's thought to spend her time brewing potions to curse the wretched Roughriders with last-quarter fumbles and to bring down upon rural Saskatchewan farming towns a continuing economic depression.

Can she be stopped? It's a question that has plagued village elders since long before the province's borders were drawn with very, very long rulers. They've tried to foil her with spears and fire and polite but firm eviction letters, but she has eluded their schemes at every turn. They've used farm animals to lure her out of the woods, and when that didn't work they placed a small child in a cage and left him out all night. Upon returning the next day, they found the child sitting outside the cage surrounded by pumpkins.

Few have tried to conquer the roguish fiend; even fewer have made it out of the thick bramble of alfalfa plants alive. Take the quiz to find out if you could be the one to finally deliver peace to the weary people of Cathedral Bluffs.

Quiz: Can You Save the Village of Cathedral Bluffs from the White Witch of Saskatoon?

1. What kind of weapons do you bring to vanquish your foe?
   a) Two machetes.
   b) A shotgun.
   c) Crossbow and flaming arrows.

2. How will you bring the witch to justice?
   a) She is not leaving the woods alive.
   b) In shackles.
   c) Ask her nicely and if she refuses I will set her hut on fire.

3. You approach the hut and all you find inside is a crying little girl. What do you do?
   a) Shoot her dead—it must be the witch in disguise!
   b) Try to comfort her.
   c) It's a trap! Run away.

4. After dealing with the little girl, you exit the hut to investigate outside. You find animal bones and the carcasses of unidentified beings. The forest has grown colder and darker. Do you stay to finish what you've started or head back to the village defeated?

   a) I will die before I bring dishonour upon my family by leaving the job incomplete.
   b) I need to sit and think for a second about my next move here.
   c) I've already started running halfway home.

5. In the darkness you hear a shuffling among the tree branches. It is the White Witch. She walks out from behind the trees with her arms up. What do you do?
   a) I approach her with my machetes drawn. I will need to bring back evidence to the villagers of her demise.
   b) I think, "Oh good. No more need for bloodshed." I ask her to kindly come forward with her arms raised so that I may shackle her and return her to the village where she will seek judgment for her crimes.
   c) I begin to cry. My pants are wet from urine and tears. The White Witch holds a finger to her lips and allows me to pass by and keep running.

Mostly As: You've been slaughtered by your enemy. She has used your weapons against you and they will never find anything of you larger than a finger. There is no escape from the White Witch.

Mostly Bs: Your lack of preparation allowed the evil hag to pounce. She has captured you and you will be kept in a cage that hangs from the tallest tree in Saskatchewan (it is also the only tree in Saskatchewan). You are mostly happy in your new home. On Fridays she brings you bread.

Mostly Cs: You've made it back to the village alive and unharmed, yet the townspeople have shunned you for your cowardice. Your spouse has turned away from you at night in bed. Your children know you are unable to keep them safe. You live out the rest of your days with the scorn of the village on your back. You are buried in the town cemetery and no one visits except for the White Witch of Saskatoon.

Get a Prince Albert Piercing in Prince Albert, Saskatchewan!

REACTIONS TO SEEING A PRINCE ALBERT PIERCING

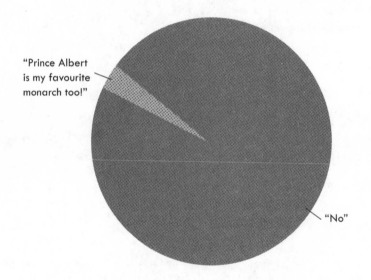

"Prince Albert is my favourite monarch too!"

"No"

Trade in a Juno

So you've won a Juno! Now what? You could either let it sit on your shelf and collect dust or trade that baby in for something of real value. Remember, it's a Juno, not a Grammy, so don't get too excited about what you might pick up for it on the award trophy black market. Nickelback has sold all 12 of their Junos for pepperoni sticks and hairspray.

Stuff You Could Get for Your Juno

- Two denim jackets
- A handful of bus tokens for the host city's transportation system
- Coupon book for your choice of Harvey's or A&W
- One six-pack of Molson but you gotta share with your friends
- A date with a member of the Barenaked Ladies (you don't get to pick who)
- Justin Bieber's pet monkey
- Three doughnut-winning Roll Up the Rim cups
- Your own comedy show on CBC
- The admiration of moms across Canada
- A *JFL* prank named after you
- Your weight in Coffee Crisp bars
- A selfie with Michael Bublé's mother
- A book deal from Penguin Random House Canada
- One coupon for half-off admission to the Toronto Zoo
- The chance to be an extra on *Degrassi*

1993 First Swollen Members song played on radio

Relate to Millennials

Teens, Canada's crankiest demographic, are experiencing more pressures as the baby boomers get closer to retirement and take all the country's money with them. The number of teens categorized as "surly" or "defiant" has increased tenfold since *Degrassi* debuted. 13% of Canadian teens didn't even want to respond to our survey because, ugh, it's like totally lame and I'm only doing this so you'll give me a ride to the mall. At Stats Canada we're interested in the issues teenagers are facing so that we may try to understand them better. Here are the 10 most common problems:

1. It's getting harder and harder to get their Zamboni licences

2. They can't find any out-of-work scientists to buy them beer

3. The White Witch of Saskatoon keeps luring them into the woods

4. Smoking weed isn't cool if everyone is doing it

5. Having a crush on the prime minister is weird

6. Grandma got put out on an ice floe

7. They keep getting lost inside Canadian Tire at their summer jobs

8. Their dad is Jeremy Bieber

9. European NHL players are stealing all their jobs

10. They can't get kissed at a MuchMusic Video Dance Party

Feel Superior to America

Ingrained in every Canadian is the ability to skate, an extraordinary tolerance for drinking, and a feeling of superiority towards Americans. Sharing a border with our friends to the south has allowed every Canadian to gently laugh at and mock American antics, including but not limited to their elections, any headline coming out of Florida, and the Kardashians. According to the most recent census of Canadian Smugness, we've compiled a list of the top 10 reasons why Canadians feel superior to Americans:

1. Free healthcare

2. International hockey tournament results

3. Canadians didn't elect George W. Bush. Twice

4. The beer is stronger

5. Ryan Gosling

6. We burned the White House down

7. Canada is younger

8. The prime minister is a babe

9. Our side of Niagara Falls is nicer

10. American preparations for a "blizzard"

Meet This Guy in Cole Harbour Who Watched Sidney Crosby Play Once

Cole Harbour, a town in Nova Scotia with a population of 25,161, is best known as the birthplace of Canada's finest hockey player and most notorious crybaby, Sidney Crosby. Founded in 1754, it has produced one elite NHL hockey player for every 100,000 grizzled fishermen.

With stats like those, there are a lot of people in Cole Harbour riding Crosby's coattails harder than Chris Kunitz. One such person is John Grant, whose claim to fame is that he watched Sidney Crosby in a game when Crosby was seven. "Yeah, I watched him play once. He was good. I knew he'd be in the NHL one day," says Grant.

Nearly 64% of Canadians claim that they too once watched a future NHLer play and knew he'd make it to the big time. Almost 23% of those Canadians think they're the reason that guy made the NHL. The 2016 census reported that 44% of Canadians believe they have a close relationship with an NHL player because they know a guy whose brother plays in the NHL, or their neighbour went to school with a guy who worked a summer with someone who played a season in the NHL.

Did You Know?

The average Canadian sees a replay of Crosby's Olympic goal every six hours.

Enjoy a PC Decadent Cookie

HOW MANY PC DECADENT COOKIES IS TOO MANY?

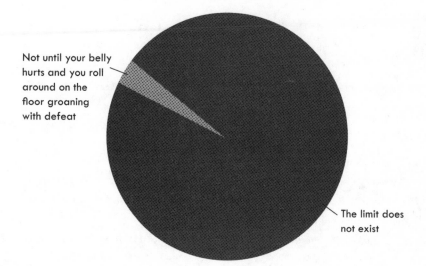

Not until your belly hurts and you roll around on the floor groaning with defeat

The limit does not exist

1997 Arctic taco forced to leave Canada

Discover How Fluent in French You Really Are

Canada has two official languages, and students begin learning French early in case they're ever in Montreal and need to know how to order off the menu. With so much classroom time spent on these lessons, many Canadians grow up to believe they're fairly fluent in French and often exaggerate their language skills on their résumé. Other common lies and exaggerations include "I completely understand French when I read it, I'm just not as good at writing it" and "Oh, she speaks with a Parisian accent and I learned Quebec French." Take this quiz to find out how fluent you actually are!

1. How do you feel about Céline Dion?
a) She did that *Titanic* song that was okay I guess.
b) Elle est ma chanteuse préféré!
c) Please, come help. My baby is trapped in the backseat of my car!

2. How long did you take French for?
a) Until I was allowed to stop taking it.
b) I minored in it at university.
c) I am an incompetent police officer and I just directed you to back into a hydrant.

3. Do you eat a lot of baguettes?
a) Actually I'm gluten-free.
b) I love bread.
c) I pretend to use hypnotism to trick pretty girls into doing silly stunts.

4. Is your favourite hockey team the Montreal Canadiens?
a) Absolutely not.
b) I was the one who lit that cop car on fire during the last riot.
c) I trick tourists into thinking I lit a cat on fire.

5. What are your feelings about *Téléfrançais*?
a) That pineapple haunts my dreams.
b) *Téléfrançais! Téléfrançais!* Bonjour! Allo! Salut!
c) I put a fake head in public toilets.

6. How cute do you think Justin Trudeau is?
a) The cutest!
b) Le plus mignon!
c) Once I spit out a live chicken in the middle of a food court.

7. Do you know what the Plains of Abraham are?

a) Ah, yes, the Plains of Abraham . . . *slowly backs away.*

b) The battle that took place on September 13, 1759. It was an important battle in the Seven Years War.

c) I dressed up as a nun and dropped a fake baby in front of a bus.

8. How many pounds of poutine do you eat a year?

a) Only when I'm drunk.

b) All my farts smell like cheese curds.

c) I dump buckets of water on elderly people and run away.

9. Have you ever been to Notre Dame Basilica?

a) No, but I saw that Disney movie once.

b) The stained glass is breathtaking.

c) I pretend to be blind and let a guide dog lead me into the lake.

10. Do you want to separate from the rest of Canada?

a) That would be disastrous.

b) I would not be opposed to it.

c) I pushed a pregnant lady into a dumpster.

Mostly As: You're probably not fluent at all. You know how to swear in French and that's about it. Most of the French words you do know came from reading cereal boxes and hearing Céline Dion songs.

Mostly Bs: Gagnant! Either you actually listened in French class or you were born in Quebec.

Mostly Cs: Zut alors! You're a mime on *Just for Laughs*. Get out of here, you scamp!

Play a Canadian Drinking Game

With the overconsumption of alcohol making up 12% of the national identity, it makes sense that Canadians would invent new ways to get intoxicated in order to do the stupid things they wanted to do while sober but were too polite to consider. Not content with international fratboy favourites like beer pong or flip cup, our nation's drinkers have made the following alcoholic games customary at every kegger and bush party across Canada:

- The Justin Bieber—Do a shot and then pee in a bucket
- Duck Duck Goose—Do a shot because someone brought two ducks and a goose to your party
- The Degrassi—Watch *Degrassi: The Next Generation* and drink every time Drake's character does something he'd be embarrassed by now
- The Nickelback—Take a slug every time you remember they exist
- The Who Can Pay the Least to Get Drunk at a Leafs Game
- Burning of Washington—Chug a beer and try to convince your friends to burn down the White House
- 2 Girls, 1 Stanley Cup—Two girls drink from the Stanley Cup
- Call Me Maybe—Drink until you feel brave enough to call your crush and ask them out
- The It's January and It's Really Cold So We're Going to Drink Because We Think That Makes You Warmer but Actually That's Not True the Alcohol Just Makes Your Blood Vessels Dilate Moving Warm Blood Closer to Your Skin Making You Feel Warmer Temporarily Game
- Century Club (Rush Version)—Put on a Rush song and take a shot of beer every minute until it ends

- The Lake Ontario—Everyone pours a bit of their alcohol into a new cup and whoever loses at beer pong has to drink this concoction. Named because it's still cleaner than water in Lake Ontario
- The Tragically Hip—Put on a Tragically Hip song and every time a small town is mentioned take a sip of your drink
- Trivial Pursuit—Drink for every question you get wrong and then drink because you feel like an idiot
- CBC—Drink a cocktail, beer, cocktail
- CFL—Drink a cocktail, do a funnel, drink liquor
- MLB—Chug a Molson, drink liquor, chug a beer
- Bob Cole—Do a shot every time Bob Cole mispronounces a player's name
- Broken Social Scene—Put on a BSS song and knock one back for every band member who appears on that song
- The Heartland—Put on an episode of *Heartland* and drink every time a horse appears onscreen
- The Jean Chrétien—Everyone takes a shot and attempts a Jean Chrétien accent. Person with worst impression takes another shot

Identify a Canadian Puck Boy

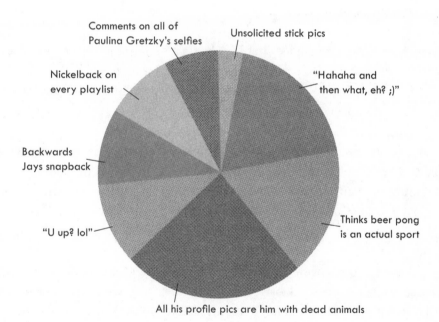

Comments on all of Paulina Gretzky's selfies

Unsolicited stick pics

Nickelback on every playlist

"Hahaha and then what, eh? ;)"

Backwards Jays snapback

"U up? lol"

Thinks beer pong is an actual sport

All his profile pics are him with dead animals

1999 Zellers Zeddy mauled by a Giant Tiger

Visit the Queen's Secret Corgi Farm

In 1983, during the height of the Cold War and Princess Diana fever, the Queen became worried about Soviet spies compromising her empire's security. The key to the future of British espionage, she believed, was to be found in her beloved corgis. Squat, intelligent, sturdy, and with loads of stamina, the corgi was deemed the perfect Trojan horse.

Corgi Spy Breed Specialties

- Able to carry top-secret messages in little satchels on their backs
- Specially trained to attack the male genital area
- Proficient in cuddles and kisses

Queen Elizabeth demanded that MI5 begin breeding the dogs in a remote Canadian location, since in 1983 few people had even heard of Canada. This changed later that year with the release of Bryan Adams's international hit single "Cuts Like a Knife."

Since the fall of 1983, Bonavista, Newfoundland, has been home to thousands of military-grade official government corgis. The operation was named "Who Let the Dogs Out." The dogs were successful in their spy training, as their large ears make them extremely effective listeners. The Queen's corgi spies are able to understand up to 1,000 phrases and commands, including "Sit," "Stay," "Fetch," "Death to the Empire," "Comrade," and "Nyet."

Although the Queen became obsessed with the idea of her beloved corgis working against Soviet Russia, a new obsession soon took her, an obsession that was more bark than bite: Princess Diana. Queen Elizabeth dropped the idea of the little spies and focused her attention on the annoyance Princess Diana was quickly becoming. With every new royal controversy, the dogs got pushed further from her mind until she forgot about the program altogether. Yet even when the Cold War ended with the fall of the Berlin Wall, the Bonavista farm continued to breed the dogs, who continued to get smarter and stealthier with every litter.

These days the farm has become something of a local tourist attraction.

The farm is able to sustain itself financially by selling the dogs' poop as manure to other farms struggling to grow crops on Newfoundland's low-quality soil and by charging admission to see the dogs and pat them on the head and give them lots of belly rubs.

Yelp Reviews

- "This place is heaven on earth for any dog lover"—doglover2137

- "Smells like poop"—sallymcknight1

- "One bit me on the genitals. 1/10. Would not visit again"—vputin52

- "We should NOT encourage animal hoarding!!!!!!!!!!!!"—PETAgirl69

Did You Know?

89% of Canadian bands break up because Jimmy quit and Jody got married.

2001 Canada regrets the Official Languages Act

Take Your Shoes Off at the Front Door

82% of Canadians think it's super weird that Americans don't take their shoes off when they walk inside someone's home. Canada is built upon such aggressively nice customs, like holding open the door and apologizing when someone bumps into you. Still, relinquishing your shoes is one of many Canadian traditions with no clear origin, such as the milk bag, Coffee Crisp, and a national love for Anne Murray. In this case, though, some exceptions apply.

Acceptable Reasons to Not Remove Your Shoes at the Door

- You're not wearing socks and you have 17 toes
- The floor is made of lava
- Your feet smell like Mike Duffy looks
- Shania Twain likes you to keep your boots under the bed
- You're allergic to good manners
- Junior's ant colony broke again
- You're in a barn
- A Canada goose is chasing you
- You came through the Polka Dot Door and can't find shoes large enough to fit your big green feet
- You live in an igloo

Learn the Differences Between Bryan and Ryan Adams

Category	Bryan Adams	Ryan Adams
Birthday	November 5, 1959	November 5, 1974
Best known song	"Summer of '69"	"Wonderwall"
Was he the one who married Mandy Moore?	No	Yup
Number of albums	14 in 36 years	14 in 16 years
What do your parents think?	They danced to "Cuts Like a Knife" at their wedding	Loved the Taylor Swift covers. Not sure about the rest of his stuff
Fashion sense	Tight T-shirt, jean jacket, spiked hair	Tight band tee, jean jacket, messy hair
Critical acclaim	Three out of five maple syrup bottles on the CBC	9.0 on Pitchfork for the *Heartbreaker* album
Is he cool?	So uncool that he then becomes cool	Tries too hard to be cool and is thus uncool
Connection to his country	As Canadian as hockey and apologies	Had the American flag on that one album cover

2003 *Electric Circus* is cancelled due to rising hydro costs

Meet the Feral Children Who Live in the West Edmonton Mall

"Where did they come from? How did they get there? What can we do about this?" These are questions that have been whispered across the province of Alberta since the discovery of the roving gangs of feral children who stealthily shuffle through the darkness of the West Edmonton Mall.

In the time-honoured Canadian tradition of avoiding anything impolite, the feral children have mainly been left to their own devices. 98% of Canadians will never even know they exist, but the 2% who do come across them will remain mentally scarred owing to their savage mind games. We've compiled a brief educational guide to these mall miscreants.

They are outfitted primarily in rags and ratty 2006 Edmonton Oilers Stanley Cup Champions T-shirts. They closely resemble extras from *Les Misérables*. You will smell them coming.

The children survive by employing a complicated bartering system involving the trading of small stolen goods for food and other tokens. No one understands why one shirt from the Gap is worth 13 loaves of bread one day and just a Joffrey Lupul hockey card the next.

Their underground society relies on a caste system that assigns every child a job based on their skills and characteristics.

The two submarines in the West Edmonton Mall make it the third largest military port in Canada.

PICKPOCKET: They craft elaborate diversions to distract you—enthralling you with their interpretive dancing or mime routine while they're reaching for your wallet. If any child approaches you in the mall, run. You will not be a victim today.

LITTLE FINGERS: They use their small, delicate hands to reach into vents and fountains to collect spare change.

HUNTER: Said to be able to take down any pigeon that accidentally flies into the mall with nothing but wits and their bare hands. For larger prey, the hunters have fashioned crude but deadly bows from materials they "found" in a Sport Chek.

GATHERER: The ferals subsist on leftovers gathered from the food court and brought back to their secret lairs. They would request that you leave more gluten-free leftovers for them, please.

UBER DRIVER: Sure, it seems sketchy to get into a Prius driven by a child, but the fare is so much cheaper than a traditional taxi and the kid gives candy to passengers. 5 stars!

Listening from the vents and the shadows, the children have learned a primitive version of English consisting mainly of hockey phrases. They find it much more comfortable to communicate using pictures of celebrities torn from abandoned tabloid magazines. Anthropologists have begun to describe this as West Edmonton Mall (WAM) Hieroglyphics:

Jennifer Aniston = sadness
Justin Bieber = disgust
Beyoncé = joy
Kim Kardashian = anger
Taylor Swift = fear

2005 Camilla, Duchess of Cornwall, nearly inherits Canada

Defend Yourself from a Canada Goose

89% of Canadians are born terrified of the Canada goose. The other 11% are lying because no Canadian goes up against the Canada goose and lives to tell the tale. The only other creature so closely associated with the nation that scares Canadians more is Justin Bieber. We've put together some dos and don'ts for anyone who encounters a Canada goose and needs to defend their life.

Do

- Play dead so that it will move on to its next target
- If you think you might cross paths with one, wear covered shoes—it will go for your toes if you have those little piggies exposed
- If you see them crossing the street and you have to bring your car to a stop to wait for them to pass, lock the doors and windows
- If you find yourself cornered by a pack, try to throw a smaller, more frightened animal (or child) in their path as a form of bait and run to safety while they maul that other being
- Watch Godzilla movies as strategic planning

Don't

- Try to outrun them. They can fly, idiot!
- Lie on the ground in a fetal position, softly whimpering
- Pee yourself! They can smell fear and are attracted to it
- Allow yourself to be outnumbered by a flock. They will exploit this weakness and attack
- Be tricked by the cuteness of the goslings. Even though their sweet little blond fuzz is sooo adorable and you could just squeeze those little cheeks, oh my God, it's behind you. It's too late for you now. It's over

Defend Your Canada Goose Jacket

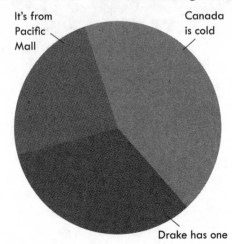

It's from Pacific Mall

Canada is cold

Drake has one

Get a Canadian Arts Council Grant

Are you seeking funding for a Canadian art project? The Canadian Arts Council wants to help! Every year the council receives thousands of applications from very creative but completely misunderstood geniuses whose gifts would be wasted if they were forced to work a boring day job like everybody else.

Here are the main steps in the process of getting a grant, from preparing your application to fulfilling your obligations as a recipient.

PRE-WORK

Step One: Spend a minimum of six weeks "finding yourself" in the British Columbia wilderness (points added for time spent in Haida Gwaii, points subtracted for time spent in Gastown, Vancouver)

Step Two: Spend a minimum of one humid summer sleeping on a couch in Montreal, working six hours per week at a coffee shop and learning no French

Step Three: Choose the perfect theme for your Tumblr

PREPARING YOUR APPLICATION

Do
- Write clearly and concisely about your intended project
- Explain how your project will bring a uniquely Canadian perspective to your discipline
- Mention at least twice how much Leonard Cohen changed your life

Don't
- Use an ugly font like Comic Sans or Papyrus
- Even think about submitting an application without first working as a surly barista or a rude record store employee
- Propose an unrealistic budget (this is Canadian art we're talking about here, buddy)

Tips
- Make your project either way too Canadian or not Canadian at all
- Ensure that your project includes something about how the Canadian landscape is cold and unforgiving
- Remember that Twitter books don't sell

POST-GRANT OBLIGATIONS

If you're lucky enough to receive a Canadian Arts Council grant, congratulations! We're excited to see what you do with your modest cheque. You've been selected as a standard-bearer of Canadian arts and culture, and a certain set of responsibilities come with the territory. Before you turn that cheque into craft beer money, you must:
- Reprogram all your radio presets to CBC Radio 2
- Develop a mild disdain for the suburbs, but an appreciation for the furniture often sold at suburban garage sales
- Purge all colour from your wardrobe
- Inform 10 strangers that you're a cyclist
- Learn to pronounce "quinoa"

2007 Tragic arcade fire kills 70 in Montreal

Become a Lacrosse Fan

One of Canada's two national sports,* lacrosse has been played on Canadian soil since long before Europeans arrived and brought with them their soft hands and fear of going into the corners. This tough, physical game originated with the Iroquois people of what would become Ontario and Quebec, and so represents the second most popular appropriation of Indigenous culture among upper-middle-class Canadians after wearing headdresses at Osheaga.

Despite the game's long history and official status, the most recent census of stick-and-ball sports reveals that relatively few Canadians actually know much about lacrosse. We're here to help.

Positions

Attackmen: Always on the offence, attackmen typically spend the entire game at the opponent's end of the field. Requiring speed and agility, they must be able to withstand brutal blows from opposing defenders and the crushing disappointment that comes with being very good at a sport few people actually watch.

Midfielders: These players roam the entire field, quickly transitioning from attack to defence. Midfielders, or "middys," are the real workhorses of the team. Since the early 1970s, however, it has been illegal to dress an actual horse for this position.

Defencemen: Those playing defence use a much longer stick in order to disrupt the opposing team's attack. Permitted to deliver bruising checks and slashes with their "long poles," they have a fearsome reputation and are often the toughest athletes who did not make their junior varsity football, baseball, basketball, or hockey teams.

Goaltender: Heavily armoured, the goaltender uses his size and stick to aggressively harass the opposing team wherever they roam. It is believed that Ron Hextall is the finest lacrosse goaltender never to have played the game. The lacrosse goaltender was briefly popularized by the movie *Air Bud 12: Paws-Checking*.

Rule Guys: In lieu of a referee, one member of each team is tasked with searching for the "rules of lacrosse" on SaskJeeves before each game. In the event of a dispute during the game, the two Rule Guys from each team skim Wikipedia until they figure it out.

Gameplay

To the untrained eye, lacrosse looks like chaos. With final scores that can typically add up to 25 or more combined goals, you could be forgiven for assuming that there's no structure to the game whatsoever. True fans, however, learn to appreciate the complexities of the game, enjoying the vicious maelstrom as one would enjoy a demolition derby or the Conservative caucus the morning after election night.

A lacrosse game lasts 60 minutes, and is divided into four quarters or two halves depending on the level of the league or the whims of the Rule Guys. The two opposing teams face off at the start

---

* The other is complaining about Gary Bettman.

of every game, quarter, and half as well as after every goal and any other interruption, such as a drunk player. In this way, the lacrosse faceoff brilliantly combines the hectic confusion of hockey with the frequent momentum-draining play stoppages of basketball. The team that wins possession of the ball attempts to fling it from stick to stick while the opposing team tries to catch it like deranged butterfly collectors. Once an attacking player gets close enough to the tiny net, they try to launch the ball forward from their stick past the helpless, flailing goalie. This repeats itself until time runs out or the coach gets frustrated and drives to the bar.

Professional Lacrosse

Although pro lacrosse salaries rank somewhere between unsuccessful YouTuber and successful Vine star, both sides of the border boast a nine-team National Lacrosse League. Often forced to play to half-empty hockey arenas whenever the local team is on a road trip, these players do not enjoy the glamorous perks that other pro athletes take for granted. The largest-ever sponsorship deal for a Canadian pro lacrosse player was a free tire rotation provided to Mark Matthews of the Saskatchewan Rush by a local mechanic in exchange for his help chasing a bat out of the garage with his lacrosse stick.

It can be a lonely life, but Canada's pro lacrosse players bravely face injuries and the injustice of being called names like "no-skates" and "faux-jock," all in hopes of lifting the Champion's Cup at the end of the season. After winning either in the playoffs or by default after all opposing teams run out of gas money, each player

on the victory squad gets to spend one day with the trophy during the off-season. Our research has uncovered the most common uses for the Cup:

- Container for collection of miniature Stanley Cups
- Fondue!
- Proving to your family that your life has worth
- Free tire rotation
- Sexy photo shoot

Trades in the NLL are illegal, which leads to a lot of disgruntled players locked in contracts and looking for ways to get out. More than two dozen Canadian lacrosse players have defected to Cuba since 2006, choosing to toil anonymously for an appreciative dictator instead of a small and disinterested fan base. Players who don't make it onto the island have been known to hide in the luggage hold of the team bus or bribe the team mascot to let them wear the costume and then make a break for freedom. Few get very far.

Lacrosse may finally gain more widespread attention and legitimacy if an effort to have it included in the summer Olympics is successful. Canada is allocating nearly 2% of its GDP to bribing the appropriate officials, and a taxpayer-funded PR campaign, "Lacrosse Is On Fleek!," is scheduled to begin later this year. If these initiatives don't work, the nation plans to give the sport back to the Indigenous population along with a sincere apology note for "taking lacrosse, and, you know, all that other stuff too."

2009 *Wild Roses* debuts and becomes Alberta's *Coronation Street*

Keep Fit and Have Fun

Canadians experience about two and a half months of nice weather each year in which it is possible to comfortably enjoy the outdoors. The remaining months are a hellscape of frost, ice, and bear attacks. This leads to a lot of time spent indoors fighting over what to watch on Canadian Netflix and whose turn it is to walk the dog. During the "summer" months it's important to squeeze in as much activity as possible so that you can feel guilt-free about your otherwise sedentary lifestyle.

Here's a list of fun Stats Canada–approved activities to get that heart rate pumping!

- Skating the Rideau Canal to escape your enemies
- Running away from a Nickelback song that your neighbour is playing too loudly
- Swimming away from your cruise ship to start a new life on a remote island
- Walking into the sea to deal with the humidity
- Watering plants for your elderly neighbour in hopes that they put you in their will
- Canoeing to get in touch with your 1/16 Aboriginal heritage
- Climbing a mountain and then screaming into the void about how much you love Céline Dion
- Mowing the lawn for your parents because they've done a lot for you and you need to show them you appreciate it
- Hiking so that you can show off on Instagram how much better you are than everyone else
- Chasing after Canada geese in the park so they know what it feels like
- Helping a friend move so that you can hold it over their head forever
- Yelling "Shoot, goddamnit" at the Ottawa Senators from the couch
- Raking leaves into a pile so that you can burn it to hide the smell of weed
- Keg stands because you deserve a treat after all these activities

Smoke Some Weed

O Canada, the true north strong and free and home to that dank stuff you've heard about from your fun uncle. Now that it's been legalized by Canada's fun babysitter, Stats Canada is not suggesting or endorsing that you partake. But if you're over the legal age and at home with lots of Jos. Louis on hand, consider this list of the best weed strains on offer.

BRITISH COLUMBIA
Baked Columbia
Tofino Crush
Redwood Stank

ALBERTA
Gretzky's Green Hands
Alberta Tar Sands
Banff Work Visa

SASKATCHEWAN
Saskatoon Hayze
Flat Gold
Saskabush Kush

MANITOBA
White Out
Polar Bear Bud
Winnipeg Weed Plant

ONTARIO
Bieber's Stratford Sativa
Superman's Kryptonite
Harvey's Hash

QUEBEC
Just for Laughs
Alouette Ounce
Trudeau's Cough

NEW BRUNSWICK
Bag of Fundy
Blaze of Glory
Ne'erbud

NOVA SCOTIA
Fisherman's Fog
Dalhousie Dank
Bluenose Dime

PRINCE EDWARD ISLAND
Phat Potato
Anne of Green Ganja
Charlottetown Red

NEWFOUNDLAND AND LABRADOR
Cannabis Cod
Stephenville Skunk
Laughing Labrador

YUKON
White Out Horse
Dawson Dawg
Yukon Gold

NORTHWEST TERRITORIES
Permafrost
Grape Slave Lake
NWTHC

NUNAVUT
Nunakush
Ice Ice Iqaluit
Ultra Ukkusiksalik

2011 Stephen Harper disappoints nation with Conservative majority government

Get a Better Phone Plan

Less than 15% of Canadians are satisfied with their cell phone plan. And with limited competition between the major carriers, the options seem to only get worse over time.

Stats Canada has polled the nation to determine usage patterns. What we've found reveals where these plans may be able to improve.

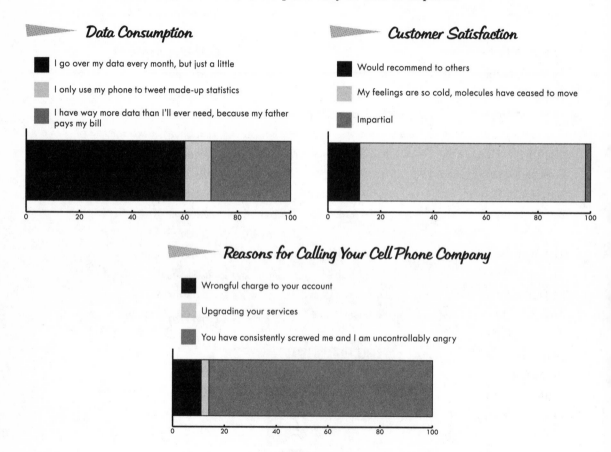

Data Consumption

■ I go over my data every month, but just a little

▢ I only use my phone to tweet made-up statistics

▨ I have way more data than I'll ever need, because my father pays my bill

Customer Satisfaction

■ Would recommend to others

▢ My feelings are so cold, molecules have ceased to move

▨ Impartial

Reasons for Calling Your Cell Phone Company

■ Wrongful charge to your account

▢ Upgrading your services

▨ You have consistently screwed me and I am uncontrollably angry

Unfortunately, the only way to fix your crap plan is to complain about it over the phone. The irony is not lost on telecom providers, we're sure.

How do you do it? Do you play dumb? Do you play hardball? What if they call your bluff and actually cancel your plan? Follow these tips and you'll be screwing Mr. Rogers in no time.

Mentally Prepare Yourself for the Call

Psyching yourself up is important. We recommend the T.E.L.U.S. method:

Tell yourself it's gonna be all right

Eat nutritiously beforehand

Lie down

Use your anger

Summon powerful emotions that have long remained dormant

Practise the Key Phrases

Have a couple of these bad boys in the chamber ready to go:

"The way I'm being treated is unacceptable"

"I've paid my bills on time for four years"

"Put me through to your mother"

"I work hard for my money so you better treat me right"

"Wind/Freedom Mobile has some good ideas"

Remember the Representative's Name

This adds a level of familiarity to the proceedings, and allows you to say things like "Listen, Jeff, we both know this data plan is bullshit" and "I'm sorry for swearing, Jeff. You're right, I may have an attitude problem."

Retention Is a Powerful Word

Congratulations, you fought hard and have finally reached the final boss, Customer Retention. The nice cousin of the Cancellation department, Customer Retention, usually a "Jenny," makes you feel as if victory is at hand. This will be the first individual you talk to who seems like a normal person, giving you a false sense of camaraderie. Don't let Jenny fool you into thinking you already have the best plan she can offer. Jenny is good at her job, but you are better. Jenny's power is literally unlimited, as far as data is concerned. Stick to the script, remember Jenny's name, and seize the phone plan that is rightfully yours.

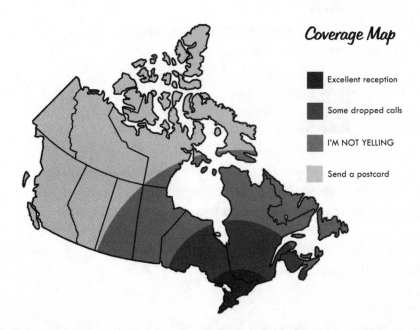

Coverage Map

- Excellent reception
- Some dropped calls
- I'M NOT YELLING
- Send a postcard

Listen to a Canadian Playlist

Canada is a country of long drives. And since radio waves can't reach many of the nation's endless highways, Canadians more than any other people depend on music playlists to stave off the boredom of an extended journey. Get into the road trip groove with these popular Canadian playlists, now available on Apple Music Canada (the same as regular Apple Music, just 30% more expensive and with half the catalogue).

- Canadian Classic Rock
- Black Coffee & Back Bacon
- Bush X Party
- Soothing Saskatchewan Slow Jams
- Pass Me a Cold One, Friend
- No Nickelback
- All Nickelback
- Justin Bieber Songs from Before He Was a Brat
- Sad Songs for When Your Team Loses
- Songs with French Lyrics So You Can Feel Cultured
- Weird Raffi
- Rad Guitar Licks for When You Realize the Arctic Is Dying
- Mennonite Mash-Ups
- Canada's Shameful Secrets
- Folk Songs to Play to Uphold This 19th Century Hipster Bullshit Aesthetic You've Got Going On
- Now That's What I Call Potato Rock! (PEI only)

Listen to One Rush Song

Rush is one of Canada's most beloved rock bands. Their songs are also very, very long. As of this writing, approximately 18% of Rush songs haven't yet ended. Here's a list of things you could do before one Rush song finishes:

- Complete Terry Fox's Marathon of Hope
- Watch all 385 episodes of *Degrassi: The Next Generation*
- Wait until the Edmonton Oilers finish their rebuild
- Talk about the weather with a coworker
- Celebrate Queen Elizabeth's 100th birthday
- Ride the Scarborough LRT
- Brew a vat of kombucha in Vancouver
- Spend winter fighting White Walkers in Nunavut
- Get brunch in Toronto
- Call your mom

Did You Know?

Canadians spend 95% of their morning figuring out if they should wear their winter or spring coat.

2013 *Stats Canada: Satire on a National Scale* released

Dress Up for Halloween

Canadian Halloween, which takes place on the third Sunday of September, is a highlight of every Canadian's year. It's an opportunity to dress up (over a snowsuit), play pranks (that do not infringe on the prank copyrights held by *Just for Laughs: Gags*), and indulge in a nearly endless bounty of Coffee Crisps, Big Turk bars, and fresh fruit from the dentist who lives two streets over. Not sure what to dress up as for the next Canadian Halloween? We've got some ideas!

- Sexy Prime Minister
- Zombie John Cabot
- Sexy Marshall McLuhan
- Newfoundland's depleted cod supply
- Sue Holloway, the first Canadian woman to compete in both the summer and winter Olympics in the same year
- Brent Butt
- Sexy Frederick Banting
- Margaret Marshall Saunders, author of the first Canadian book to sell more than 1,000,000 copies
- One of the horses from CBC's *Heartland*
- Sexy Louis Riel
- Marilyn Bell, the first person to swim across Lake Ontario
- Zombie *Titanic* passenger
- Sexy Parliament Building
- Normal Stephen Harper
- Roberta Bondar, Canada's first female astronaut
- Sexy Bay Blanket
- Bertha Wilson, the first woman justice of the Supreme Court
- Sexy Wendel Clark
- Eileen Tallman, organizer of the first Canadian bank strike

Meet Ogopogo

Name: Ogopogo • **Birthplace:** Okanagan Lake, British Columbia • **Age:** 91, but lies about it!

Likes: Long swims alongside the beach, moonlit swims, eating children who get too far from the shore, the intimacy that comes when you really get to know a person, watching cooking shows, wine, terrorizing tourists out for a swim, the way rain smells, travel

Dislikes: Being compared to her older sister Nelly, liars, cheaters, when the townspeople carry torches and spears to the lake to try to catch the lake monster that has been eating their children, when guys wear pinky rings, the patriarchy

British Columbia Provincial Police	Zed-Files Dept. of Strange Crimes	British Columbia Provincial Police

WANTED
FOR EATING CHILDREN

Ogopogo / Female / Green

Anyone with valuable information on the whereabouts
of Ogopogo please immediately contact
Det. <u>DAVID DUCHOVNY</u>

2015 José Bautista disrespects baseball by throwing bat

Check Out Michael Cera's Speed Dial

SPEED DIAL   RECENTS   CONTACTS

Search people & places

M Moustache Barber — Work

J Jonah Hill — Mobile

B Beanie Baby Appraiser — Work

U Ukulele Repair Man — Mobile

V VHS 4 Rent — Work

G Grandpapa's Stylist — Work

MICHAEL CERA'S SPEED DIAL

Learn About Justin Trudeau's Alternative Careers

Justin Trudeau is a politician, McGill University graduate, and father, but he's so much more than that. He's also ridiculously good-looking. But what would he be if he weren't our leader? Here are some other career paths that Canada's favourite son could have pursued:

- Hunky ski instructor
- Hunky pool boy
- Hunky Roots model
- Hunky yoga instructor
- Hunky women's studies professor at McGill
- Hunky Property Brother
- Hunky neighbourhood dad who coaches his kid's hockey team
- Hunky dog walker
- Hunky aging member of a popular Canadian boy band circa 2000
- Hunky dude who works at the weed dispensary

Did You Know?

Justin Trudeau has formed a bromance with 45% of world leaders.

2017 American refugees flood Canadian border

Take the Quiz:
How Canadian Are You?

Check all the boxes that apply!

☐ Slipped on ice while changing the Shania Twain song on your phone

☐ Drove past three Starbucks to go to a Tim Hortons

☐ Defended Céline Dion from trolls online who have no idea what good music is

☐ Cried when your hockey team lost in the playoffs

☐ Cried when your hockey team won in the playoffs

☐ Cared about basketball for two weeks when the Raptors were in the playoffs

☐ Went somewhere on vacation and made friends with the only other Canadians at the resort

☐ Remember where you were when Crosby scored the Golden Goal

☐ Woke up at 5 a.m. To watch the gold medal hockey game during the Sochi Olympics

☐ Felt proud of Justin Bieber

☐ Felt embarrassed by Justin Bieber

☐ Felt unsure about how to feel about Justin Bieber

☐ Felt you've spent too much time thinking about Justin Bieber

☐ Had to explain to an American that, no, you don't know their friend John in Vancouver

☐ Still hope that Ryan Gosling and Rachel McAdams will figure it out

☐ Have watched an awards show and pointed out all the Canadians

☐ Have counted all the Canadian hockey players on American teams during the playoffs and explained that really it's a win for Canada

☐ Fantasized about punching Gary Bettman

☐ Have actually punched Gary Bettman

☐ Have spent more than 15 minutes talking to a foreigner about the weather in Canada

☐ Have been an extra on *Degrassi*

☐ Have worn a wool cardigan in August

☐ Have worn shorts in February

☐ Have apologized when someone has bumped into you

- [ ] Explained why Alanis Morissette's song "Ironic" actually is ironic

- [ ] Pointed out movies set in New York that were actually filmed in Toronto

- [ ] Own every variation of the red Canada mittens

- [ ] Lost at least one mitten from every pair of red Canada mittens

- [ ] Hoped Tessa Virtue and Scott Moir would get together

- [ ] Skated the Rideau Canal while eating a Beaver Tail

- [ ] Ate poutine while drunk

- [ ] Related to an episode of *Corner Gas*

- [ ] Been Screeched

- [ ] Couldn't leave your house because there was some form of wildlife at your door

- [ ] Drank out of the Stanley Cup

- [ ] Learned how to say "sorry" in other languages to help you when travelling

- [ ] Have a tattoo of your hockey team's logo

- [ ] Cheered against the Canucks in the 2011 Stanley Cup finals

- [ ] Found maple syrup on your hands even though you haven't eaten anything with maple syrup

- [ ] Have ordered a panini at Tim Hortons and it's been burnt

- [ ] Have won the meat raffle at a Manitoba Social

- [ ] Have returned more than $100 worth of empties in a single trip

- [ ] Have racked up a $100 "roaming" bill without even leaving the country

- [ ] Have sat in the bed of a pickup truck travelling at highway speeds

- [ ] Have waited more than four hours for a ferry boat

- [ ] Have used your backyard as a secondary beer fridge in the winter

- [ ] Have made Kraft Dinner on a hotplate

Conclusion: Save Canada

As the nation celebrates its 150th anniversary, the future of liberal democracies like Canada may be at risk. In the United Kingdom, the stunning #Brexit vote resulted in citizens turning their backs on the dream of a united Europe, and closing the door to the nation until it was barely open enough to admit talented foreign soccer players. Closer to home, the United States elected Donald Trump, a dangerous nationalist whose campaign was built around fear, hats, and words you haven't heard since grandpa died. Everywhere you look, the values that many Canadians hold dear to their hearts—tolerance, cooperation, and a love of foreign food *and* foreign people—seem to be disappearing.

Are you concerned about Canada making some sort of rash decision that will poison the political landscape and sour relations with the global community? Here are some warning signs to look out for:

- Alberta calling for a total and complete shutdown of foreign beef entering the west
- Unemployment rate in your town exceeds the unemployment rate in Windsor
- Nunavut begins minting own currency
- China purchases most of Saskatchewan
- Canada builds a wall and makes Minnesota pay for it
- An overwhelming distrust in government and your neighbours
- The west's problems getting blamed on east coast migrants
- Quebec actually trying to secede from the nation

Additional warning signs will not be as obvious, and may spring up where you least expect: an errant comment about NAFTA from your uncle at Thanksgiving, a protest sign that's not in both official languages, or a Conservative MP elected in Downtown Toronto—all signs pointing to a country on the edge.

What can you do as a Canadian to prevent our own version of democratic collapse?

- Report any anti-cheese curd rhetoric on Facebook
- Talk to a Canadian who lives more than 10 km away from a city
- Spend 0% of your time committing hate crimes, vandalizing houses of worship, or perpetuating conspiracies online
- Write your MP and demand that they keep an eye on Stephen Harper, retired or not
- Hug a refugee

It may feel like the world is hurtling towards an uncertain and frightening future, with once-solid institutions crumbling under the weight of populist uprisings, but this may be Canada's opportunity to lead the globe back to peaceful stability. We are more than just a nation of mediocre-coffee drinkers and better-than-average winter drivers. We're defined by a spirit more resilient than the third-line winger who always gives it 110%, more inclusive than the chicken fingers and chop suey at the Mandarin Buffet, and more stubbornly optimistic than the guy who wears shorts in March. We will not be led down the path of suspicion and exclusion. We will not turn on each other, and we will set an example for all other nations to follow.

On our great nation's 150th birthday, give your fellow citizens the greatest gift of all: being as Canadian as you damn well can be.

Acknowledgments

Andrew, Julia, Sam, and Eric would like to thank everyone who helped us turn this dumb joke into not one but two actual honest-to-goodness, printed-on-Canadian-softwood-paper books. First and foremost, special thanks goes to Justin Stoller at Penguin Random House for his patient and helpful encouragement throughout this process; to the book's designer, Leah Springate; and to our agent, Carly Watters at P.S. Literary. A great big Canadian thank you also goes to everybody who follows us on Twitter, especially those that took the time to answer our census—your stories about your particular corners of this great nation were invaluable and helped us learn so much about the people and places that lie beyond Toronto's city limits. And finally, each of us would like to thank the parents, siblings, and partners who put up with all the dumb jokes we make for free, and for encouraging us to do it professionally for $0.11 Canadian per copy sold.

Art Credits

Half title, Title page, Part opener, Acknowledgments car: CSA Images/Getty Images

Page ii moose: Flickr/Internet Archive Book Images/ In pine-tree jungles: a handbook for sportsmen and campers in the great Maine woods, 1902

Page vi bear: FreeVector.com [link https://www. freevector.com/bear-illustration]

Page xii moose: CSA Images/Getty Images

Page xi elk and beaver: Flickr/The British Library/ Primary Geography. [With Illustrations], 1894

Page 7 suitcase: Flickr/Internet Archive Book Images/Catalogue no. 16, spring/summer/R. H. Macy & Co.

Page 20 lighthouse: Flickr/Internet Archive Book Images/Sessional papers of the Dominion of Canada 1911, 1911

Page 23 record: Freevector.com [https://www. freevector.com/vintage-music-images]

Page 52 bike: Flickr/The British Library/A wheel to Moscow and back. The record of a record cycle ride, 1895

Pages 58–59 beer caps: vecteezy.com/© nightwolf-dezines [https://www.vecteezy.com/ vector-art/82194-free-vector-beer-and-juices-bottle-caps]

Page 60 peace: publicdomainpictures.net. [http:// www.publicdomainpictures.net/view-image. php?image=78210&picture=peace-sign]

Pages 70–71 dinosaur bones: Flickr/The British Library/Manual of Geology: treating of the

principles of the science with special reference to American geological history ... Revised edition, 1895

Page 74 bison: Flickr/Internet Archive Book Images/ Iconographie du règne animal de G. Cuvier, ou, Représentation d'après nature de l'une des espèces les plus et souvent non encore figurées de chaque genre d'animaux : avec un texte descriptif mis au courant de la science : ouvrage pouvant servir d'atlas a tous les traites de zoologie, 1829

Page 75 polar bear: Flickr/The British Library/ Amerika: eine allgemeine Landeskunde. In Gemeinschaft mit Dr. E. Deckert und Prof. Dr. W. Kükenthal herausgegeben von Prof. Dr. W. Sievers. Mit 201 Abbildungen, etc., 1894

Page 77 polar bear: Flickr/The British Library/ Nimrod of the North, or hunting and fishing adventures in the Arctic regions, 1885

Page 80 crown: Flickr/Internet Archive Book Images/Heraldry, historical and popular, 1864

Page 81 umbrella: Flickr/Internet Archive Book Images/Atlanta City Directory, 1913

Page 95 lady doing her nails: © Retro Clipart | Dreamstime.com

Page 113 fish: Flickr/Internet Archive Book Images/ Iconographie du règne animal de G. Cuvier, ou, Représentation d'après nature de l'une des espèces les plus et souvent non encore figurées de chaque genre d'animaux : avec un texte descriptif mis au courant de la science : ouvrage pouvant servir d'atlas a tous les traites de zoologie, 1829